Mastering WordPress:

A Comprehensive Guide to Building Dynamic Websites for Beginners and Small Business Owners

Lewis Finan

Table of Contents

Introduction 8

Chapter 1: Understanding WordPress and Its Benefits 12

    1.1 Setting Up Your WordPress Environment.............................15

    1.2 Navigating the WordPress Dashboard 19

    1.3 Getting Started with WordPress 24

Chapter 2: Installing WordPress on Your Hosting Server 30

    2.1 Exploring Themes and Customizing Your Site.....................34

    2.2 Creating and Managing User Accounts................................38

    2.3 Building Your Website's Foundation....................................42

Chapter 3: Planning Your Website's Structure and Layout..........47

    3.1 Creating Pages and Organizing Content 50

    3.1 Creating Pages and Organizing Content 54

    3.2 Configuring Essential Plugins for Functionality....................58

    3.3 Designing Your Website 62

Chapter 4: Choosing the Right Theme for Your Business 67

    4.1 Customizing Your Website's Appearance 71

    4.2 Incorporating Images and Media 76

    4.3 Enhancing Your Website's Functionality 80

Chapter 5: Enhancing Your Website's Functionality...................86

    5.1 Optimizing Your Website for Search Engines 90

    5.2 Implementing E-commerce Functionality............................95

    5.3 Maintaining and Securing Your Website 101

Chapter 6: Backing Up and Restoring Your WordPress Site 107

    6.1 Updating WordPress, Themes, and Plugins.........................112

    6.2 Implementing Security Measures and Best Practices............116

    6.3 Growing Your Website and Engaging Your Audience 121

Chapter 7: Utilizing Social Media Integration 126

    7.1 Implementing Effective Content Marketing Strategies 131

    7.2 Analyzing Website Performance and Making Improvements 135

7.3 Troubleshooting and Support...140

Chapter 8: Common WordPress Issues and Solutions............................145

8.1 Seeking Help from the WordPress Community 148

8.2 Engaging Professional WordPress Support Services........................153

Conclusion 158

Recap of Key Concepts: 160

Next Steps in Mastering WordPress:...162

Introduction:

In today's digital age, having a strong online presence is crucial for individuals and small businesses alike. Websites serve as virtual storefronts, providing a platform to showcase products, services, and ideas to a global audience. However, building a website from scratch can be a daunting task, especially for beginners who may not possess extensive technical knowledge.

"Mastering WordPress: A Comprehensive Guide to Building Dynamic Websites for Beginners and Small Business Owners" is a comprehensive resource designed to empower individuals and small business owners with the necessary skills to create professional and dynamic websites with ease. Whether you're starting a blog, establishing an online portfolio, or launching an e-commerce store, this book serves as your trusted companion on the journey to WordPress mastery.

Written with clarity and accessibility in mind, this guide demystifies the intricacies of WordPress, the world's most popular content management system (CMS). With its intuitive interface, extensive plugin library, and a vast array of themes, WordPress provides a solid foundation for website creation, regardless of your technical expertise. By following the step-by-step instructions and real-world examples presented in this book, you'll gain the confidence and proficiency needed to harness WordPress's full potential.

Inside "Mastering WordPress," you'll find:

1. An introduction to WordPress: Discover the fundamentals of WordPress, including its features, advantages, and the reasons behind its widespread adoption.

2. Setting up your website: Learn how to register a domain name, choose a hosting provider, and install WordPress. You'll also explore essential configuration settings to optimize your site's performance and security.

3. Navigating the WordPress dashboard: Gain a comprehensive understanding of the WordPress dashboard and its various sections. From creating pages and posts to managing media files, you'll become well-versed in handling the core elements of your website.

4. Customizing your website's appearance: Dive into the world of WordPress themes and explore different customization options to give your site a unique look and feel. Discover how to modify headers, footers, sidebars, and menus to align with your branding.

5. Extending functionality with plugins: Unleash the power of WordPress plugins to enhance your website's functionality. From search engine optimization (SEO) and social media integration to e-commerce and contact forms, you'll learn how to select and configure plugins to meet your specific needs.

6. Creating dynamic content: Master the art of crafting compelling and engaging content using WordPress's built-in editor. Explore formatting options, multimedia integration, and best practices for structuring blog posts and pages.

7. Optimizing your website for search engines: Learn effective techniques for improving your website's visibility in search engine results. Discover how to optimize keywords, meta tags, and URLs to attract organic traffic and maximize your online reach.

8. Securing your website: Understand the importance of website security and discover essential practices to protect your WordPress site from potential threats. From implementing strong passwords to regularly updating plugins, you'll learn how to safeguard your website and user data.

9. Website maintenance and performance optimization: Discover strategies to keep your website running smoothly and efficiently. Learn about regular backups, database optimization, caching, and other techniques to ensure optimal performance.

"Mastering WordPress: A Comprehensive Guide to Building Dynamic Websites for Beginners and Small Business Owners" equips you with the knowledge and skills needed to embark on your WordPress journey confidently. By the end of this book, you'll have the ability to create stunning, functional, and user-friendly websites that effectively communicate your message and help you achieve your online goals. Let's dive into the world of WordPress and unlock the endless possibilities of web development!

Chapter 1: Understanding WordPress and Its Benefits

In today's digital landscape, having a strong online presence is essential for individuals and businesses alike. A website serves as a virtual storefront, a platform to showcase products, services, and ideas to a global audience. However, building a website from scratch can be a daunting task, requiring technical expertise and coding knowledge. This is where WordPress comes into play. WordPress is the world's most popular content management system (CMS), offering a user-friendly interface and powerful features that make website creation accessible to beginners and professionals alike. In this article, we will explore WordPress in-depth, understanding its core principles and highlighting its numerous benefits.

What is WordPress?

WordPress is an open-source CMS that powers more than 40% of the websites on the internet today. It was initially developed as a blogging platform in 2003 but has evolved into a versatile CMS that allows users to create various types of websites, including blogs, business websites, e-commerce stores, portfolios, and more. WordPress is built on PHP and MySQL, providing a flexible and customizable platform for web development.

The Benefits of WordPress:

1. User-Friendly Interface: One of the main reasons behind WordPress's popularity is its intuitive and user-friendly interface.

You don't need to be a coding expert to create and manage a WordPress website. The interface is designed to be beginner-friendly, allowing users to easily navigate through various sections and perform tasks such as adding content, installing themes and plugins, and customizing the website's appearance.

2. Customization Options: WordPress offers a wide range of themes and templates that enable users to customize the look and feel of their websites. Whether you want a professional and sleek design or a creative and vibrant layout, there are thousands of free and premium themes available. Additionally, WordPress allows for easy customization of headers, footers, menus, and sidebars, giving you full control over your website's design.

3. Extensive Plugin Library: Plugins are one of the key features that make WordPress so powerful. Plugins are add-ons that extend the functionality of your website. With over 58,000 plugins available in the official WordPress plugin directory, you can enhance your website with features such as contact forms, e-commerce capabilities, social media integration, search engine optimization (SEO), analytics, and much more. The plugin architecture is easy to understand and allows users to install, activate, and configure plugins with just a few clicks.

4. SEO-Friendly: Search engine optimization is crucial for driving organic traffic to your website. WordPress is inherently SEO-friendly, providing features and tools that help improve your website's visibility in search engine rankings. WordPress generates clean and semantic code, has built-in support for metadata, and allows for easy integration with popular SEO plugins. These features enable users to optimize their website's content, meta tags, and URLs, improving their chances of ranking higher in search results.

5. Responsive and Mobile-Friendly: With the increasing use of smartphones and tablets, it's essential for websites to be responsive

and mobile-friendly. WordPress themes are designed to be responsive by default, ensuring that your website adapts seamlessly to different screen sizes and devices. This allows for a consistent user experience across desktops, laptops, smartphones, and tablets, catering to the needs of your audience.

6. E-Commerce Capabilities: WordPress, in combination with plugins like WooCommerce, provides a robust platform for building e-commerce websites. WooCommerce is the most popular e-commerce plugin for WordPress, offering features such as product listings, shopping cart functionality, secure payment gateways, inventory management, and order tracking. This makes it easier than ever for small businesses to set up and manage their online stores.

7. Active Community and Support: WordPress has a vibrant and active community of developers, designers, and users who contribute to its growth and development. The WordPress community provides support through forums, documentation, tutorials, and meetups, making it easier for users to find solutions to their queries and learn from others' experiences. The constant updates and improvements to WordPress ensure that users have access to a stable and secure platform.

WordPress has revolutionized the world of web development, making it accessible to beginners and small business owners. Its user-friendly interface, customization options, extensive plugin library, SEO-friendliness, responsiveness, e-commerce capabilities, and strong community support are just a few of the many benefits that have contributed to its immense popularity. Whether you're a blogger, a freelancer, or a business owner, WordPress provides a powerful and flexible platform to create dynamic and engaging websites. By harnessing the power of WordPress, you can establish a strong online presence, reach your target audience, and achieve your digital goals.

1.1 Setting Up Your WordPress Environment

Before diving into the exciting world of WordPress website creation, it's crucial to set up a proper environment that facilitates a smooth and efficient workflow. This involves selecting a reliable hosting provider, registering a domain name, and installing WordPress. In this article, we will guide you through the process of setting up your WordPress environment, ensuring that you have a solid foundation to build upon.

1. Choosing a Hosting Provider:

A hosting provider is a company that stores your website files and makes them accessible to the internet. Selecting a reliable hosting provider is essential for the performance, security, and scalability of your WordPress website. Consider the following factors when choosing a hosting provider:

a. Reliability and Uptime: Look for a hosting provider with a track record of high uptime, ensuring that your website remains accessible to visitors around the clock.
b. Performance and Speed: Opt for a hosting provider that offers fast server response times and employs caching mechanisms to optimize website loading speed.
c. Scalability: As your website grows, you may require additional resources. Choose a hosting provider that allows for easy scalability to accommodate increased traffic and data.
d. Security: Ensure that the hosting provider offers robust security measures, including regular backups, firewalls, and SSL certificates, to protect your website from potential threats.

e. Customer Support: Reliable customer support is essential in case you encounter any issues or have questions. Look for a hosting provider that offers 24/7 support through various channels.

2. Registering a Domain Name:

A domain name is the web address that visitors will use to access your website (e.g., www.yourwebsite.com). When choosing a domain name, consider the following tips:

a. Relevance and Branding: Select a domain name that reflects your website's purpose or your brand. It should be memorable and easy to type.
b. Keywords: If possible, include relevant keywords in your domain name to improve search engine optimization (SEO).
c. Domain Extension: Choose a domain extension that aligns with your website's purpose (.com, .org, .net, etc.). The .com extension is generally recommended for commercial websites.
d. Availability: Check the availability of your desired domain name using domain registration services. If your preferred name is unavailable, consider alternative options or use domain name generators for ideas.
e. Registration: Once you've found an available domain name, register it with a reputable domain registrar. Some hosting providers offer domain registration services as well, simplifying the process.

3. Installing WordPress:

After securing your hosting provider and domain name, it's time to install WordPress. Most hosting providers offer a simple one-click installation process for WordPress. Follow these steps:

a. Access your hosting provider's control panel or dashboard. Look for an option like "Install WordPress" or "WordPress Installer."
b. Select the domain where you want to install WordPress. If you have multiple domains, choose the appropriate one.
c. Choose a directory for your WordPress installation. If you want your website to appear on the root domain (e.g., www.yourwebsite.com), leave the directory field blank. Otherwise, specify a directory name (e.g., /blog) to create a subdirectory for your WordPress installation.
d. Set up an admin username and password. These credentials will be used to access your WordPress dashboard, so choose a strong password for security purposes.
e. Enter your website's title and a brief description. This information will appear in search engine results and on your website.
f. Complete the installation process and wait for the confirmation message.

4. Configuring Basic WordPress Settings:

Once WordPress is installed, it's essential to configure some basic settings for your website:

a. Accessing the WordPress Dashboard: To access the WordPress dashboard, go to your domain name followed by "/wp-admin" (e.g., www.yourwebsite.com/wp-admin). Enter your admin username and password to log in.

b. General Settings: In the dashboard, navigate to "Settings" > "General." Here, you can set your website's title and tagline. You can also modify the site's URL structure, time zone, and other general settings.

c. Permalinks: Permalinks determine the structure of URLs for your website's pages and posts. Go to "Settings" > "Permalinks" and choose a permalink structure that is user-friendly and SEO-friendly. Common options include the post name, category/hostname, and custom structures.

d. User Registration: Depending on your website's purpose, you may want to allow user registration. In "Settings" > "General," check the "Membership" or "Anyone can register" box if you want to enable user registration.

e. Discussion Settings: If your website includes a blog and you want to enable comments, go to "Settings" > "Discussion" and configure the comment settings according to your preferences.

f. Media Settings: Determine the default sizes for images uploaded to your website in "Settings" > "Media." Adjust the dimensions to fit your website's design and layout.

Setting up your WordPress environment correctly is essential for a successful website creation journey. Choose a reliable hosting provider, register a domain name that reflects your brand, and install WordPress using the provided tools. Configure the basic settings to align with your website's goals and requirements. By following these steps, you'll establish a solid foundation for building a dynamic and engaging WordPress website.

1.2 Navigating the WordPress Dashboard

The WordPress dashboard is the control center of your website, where you can manage and customize various aspects of your WordPress site. It provides a user-friendly interface that allows you to create and edit pages, publish blog posts, manage media files, install plugins and themes, and much more. Navigating the WordPress dashboard effectively is essential for efficiently managing your website and maximizing its potential. In this article, we will explore the different sections and features of the WordPress dashboard, empowering you to navigate and utilize its functionalities with ease.

Accessing the WordPress Dashboard:

To access the WordPress dashboard, follow these simple steps:

1. Enter the URL of your website in the browser's address bar (e.g., www.yourwebsite.com).
2. Add "/wp-admin" at the end of the URL (e.g., www.yourwebsite.com/wp-admin).
3. Press Enter to load the login page.
4. Enter your admin username and password that you set during the WordPress installation process.
5. Click the "Log In" button to access the WordPress dashboard.

Understanding the WordPress Dashboard Layout:

Upon logging into the WordPress dashboard, you'll be greeted with the default layout, which consists of several key sections. Let's explore each section in detail:

1. **Admin Bar**: The admin bar appears at the top of the screen when you're logged in as an administrator. It provides quick access to various administrative tasks, such as adding new posts, creating new pages, managing comments, and accessing your website's front end.

2. **Sidebar Menu**: The sidebar menu is located on the left-hand side of the screen and serves as the primary navigation for the WordPress dashboard. It provides access to all the major sections and features of WordPress. The menu items include Dashboard, Posts, Media, Pages, Comments, Appearance, Plugins, Users, Tools, and Settings. Hovering over each menu item reveals sub-menus with additional options.

3. **Admin Dashboard**: The admin dashboard is the default landing page of the WordPress dashboard. It provides an overview of your website's activity, including recent posts, comments, and site statistics. You can customize the dashboard by adding or removing widgets to suit your preferences.

4. **Screen Options**: Located in the top-right corner of the dashboard, the "Screen Options" tab allows you to control the visibility of specific elements on the screen. By clicking on it, you can toggle the display of various sections and customize the layout according to your needs.

Exploring Key Dashboard Sections and Features:

Now that we have a general understanding of the WordPress dashboard layout, let's delve into the key sections and features you'll encounter:

1. **Posts**: The "Posts" section allows you to create, edit, and manage blog posts. You can add new posts, categorize them, assign tags, set featured images, and manage comments. The "Categories" and "Tags" sub-menus under "Posts" enables you to create and manage categories and tags for organizing your blog content.

2. **Media**: The "Media" section is where you can upload, manage, and organize your media files, including images, videos, and audio files. You can add media directly to your posts and pages or create galleries. The "Library" sub-menu allows you to view and edit existing media files.

3. **Pages**: The "Pages" section is where you can create and manage static pages, such as the About page, Contact page, or any other content that doesn't fall into the blog post category. You can create hierarchical structures, set featured images, and customize page templates.

4. **Comments**: The "Comments" section allows you to moderate and manage comments on your blog posts. You can approve, delete, or reply to comments. WordPress provides spam filters and moderation settings to help you maintain a healthy comment section.

5. **Appearance**: The "Appearance" section is where you can customize the visual aspects of your website. This includes selecting and customizing themes, creating menus and navigation structures, managing widgets, and accessing the theme editor to modify the underlying code.

6. **Plugins**: The "Plugins" section is where you can install, activate, deactivate, and manage plugins. Plugins extend the functionality of your WordPress website and offer features like contact forms, SEO optimization, social media integration, and much more. You can also access plugin settings and configure their behavior through this section.

7. **Users**: The "Users" section allows you to manage user accounts and roles. You can add new users, assign them roles (such as Administrator, Editor, Author, etc.), and control their permissions. This section also enables you to edit your own user profile and change your password.

8. **Tools**: The "Tools" section provides various utilities to assist in managing your WordPress site. This includes importing and exporting content, managing site backups, and accessing the site's health and security features.

9. **Settings**: The "Settings" section is where you can configure the general settings for your website. It includes options for site title and tagline, permalink structure, reading settings, discussion settings, media settings, and much more. Each sub-menu within the "Settings" section focuses on a specific aspect of your site's configuration.

Customizing the WordPress Dashboard:

WordPress allows you to customize the dashboard to suit your preferences and workflow. Here are some customization options:

1. **Screen Options**: As mentioned earlier, the "Screen Options" tab allows you to show or hide specific elements on the screen. You

can toggle the visibility of widgets, meta boxes, and other dashboard components.

2. **Drag-and-Drop Widgets**: The admin dashboard is composed of customizable widgets that provide at-a-glance information. You can rearrange the widgets by dragging and dropping them into different positions. Additionally, you can add new widgets or remove existing ones using the "+ Add" or "Screen Options" buttons.

3. **User Roles and Permissions**: By default, WordPress provides different user roles with varying levels of access and permissions. You can modify these roles or create custom roles to define the capabilities of each user on your site.

4. **Admin Color Scheme**: WordPress offers different admin color schemes to personalize the appearance of the dashboard. You can choose a color scheme that suits your preferences by going to "Users" > "Your Profile" and selecting a scheme under "Admin Color Scheme."

Navigating the WordPress dashboard is crucial for efficiently managing your website and leveraging its full potential. By understanding the layout, sections, and features of the dashboard, you can confidently create and edit posts, manage media, install plugins, customize themes, and configure settings. Take advantage of the customization options available to tailor the dashboard to your workflow and preferences. With a solid grasp of the WordPress dashboard, you'll be empowered to build and maintain a dynamic and successful website.

1.3 Getting Started with WordPress

WordPress is a popular and powerful content management system (CMS) that allows you to create and manage websites without extensive coding knowledge. It provides a user-friendly interface, a vast library of themes and plugins, and a strong community support system. Whether you're a blogger, a small business owner, or an aspiring web developer, getting started with WordPress is a great way to establish an online presence and showcase your content or products. In this guide, we will walk you through the essential steps to get started with WordPress, from installing WordPress to creating your first website.

Step 1: Choosing a Hosting Provider:

The first step in getting started with WordPress is selecting a hosting provider. A hosting provider stores your website files and makes them accessible on the internet. Consider the following factors when choosing a hosting provider:

1. Reliability and Uptime: Look for a hosting provider with a track record of high uptime, ensuring that your website remains accessible to visitors.
2. Performance and Speed: Opt for a hosting provider that offers fast server response times and employs caching mechanisms to optimize website loading speed.
3. Scalability: As your website grows, you may require additional resources. Choose a hosting provider that allows for easy scalability to accommodate increased traffic and data.

4. Security: Ensure that the hosting provider offers robust security measures, including regular backups, firewalls, and SSL certificates, to protect your website from potential threats.
5. Customer Support: Reliable customer support is essential in case you encounter any issues or have questions. Look for a hosting provider that offers 24/7 support through various channels.

Step 2: Registering a Domain Name:

After selecting a hosting provider, the next step is to register a domain name. A domain name is the web address that visitors will use to access your website (e.g., www.yourwebsite.com). Consider the following tips when choosing a domain name:

1. Relevance and Branding: Select a domain name that reflects your website's purpose or your brand. It should be memorable and easy to type.
2. Keywords: If possible, include relevant keywords in your domain name to improve search engine optimization (SEO).
3. Domain Extension: Choose a domain extension that aligns with your website's purpose (.com, .org, .net, etc.). The .com extension is generally recommended for commercial websites.
4. Availability: Check the availability of your desired domain name using domain registration services. If your preferred name is unavailable, consider alternative options or use domain name generators for ideas.
5. Registration: Once you've found an available domain name, register it with a reputable domain registrar. Some hosting providers offer domain registration services as well, simplifying the process.

Step 3: Installing WordPress:

After securing a hosting provider and a domain name, it's time to install WordPress. Most hosting providers offer a simple one-click installation process for WordPress. Follow these steps:

1. Access your hosting provider's control panel or dashboard. Look for an option like "Install WordPress" or "WordPress Installer."
2. Select the domain where you want to install WordPress. If you have multiple domains, choose the appropriate one.
3. Choose a directory for your WordPress installation. If you want your website to appear on the root domain (e.g., www.yourwebsite.com), leave the directory field blank. Otherwise, specify a directory name (e.g., /blog) to create a subdirectory for your WordPress installation.
4. Set up an admin username and password. These credentials will be used to access your WordPress dashboard, so choose a strong password for security purposes.
5. Enter your website's title and a brief description. This information will appear in search engine results and on your website.
6. Complete the installation process and wait for the confirmation message.

Step 4: Configuring Basic Settings:

After installing WordPress, you'll need to configure some basic settings to personalize your website. Access your WordPress dashboard by appending "/wp-admin" to your domain name (e.g., www.yourwebsite.com/wp-admin). Here are some key settings to consider:

1. General Settings: Navigate to "Settings" > "General" to set your website's title and tagline. You can also modify the site's URL structure, time zone, and other general settings.
2. Permalinks: Permalinks determine the structure of URLs for your website's pages and posts. Go to "Settings" > "Permalinks" and choose a permalink structure that is user-friendly and SEO-friendly.
3. User Registration: Depending on your website's purpose, you may want to allow user registration. In "Settings" > "General," check the "Membership" or "Anyone can register" box if you want to enable user registration.
4. Discussion Settings: If your website includes a blog and you want to enable comments, go to "Settings" > "Discussion" and configure the comment settings according to your preferences.
5. Media Settings: Determine the default sizes for images uploaded to your website in "Settings" > "Media." Adjust the dimensions to fit your website's design and layout.

Step 5: Choosing a Theme and Customizing Your Website:

WordPress offers a wide range of themes that control the appearance and layout of your website. Here's how to choose and customize a theme:

1. Access the "Appearance" section in your WordPress dashboard and click on "Themes."

2. Browse through the available themes and select one that suits your website's purpose and design preferences.
3. Install and activate the chosen theme. You can preview how your website will look with the theme before activating it.
4. Customize the theme by accessing the "Customize" option. Here, you can modify various elements such as colors, fonts, header and footer, menus, and widgets.
5. Experiment with different customization options to achieve the desired look and feel for your website.

Step 6: Adding Content and Functionality:

With your WordPress website set up and customized, it's time to start adding content and functionality:

1. Creating Pages and Posts: Use the "Pages" section to create essential pages like Home, About, Contact, and any other relevant pages. The "Posts" section is where you can publish blog posts.
2. Customizing Menus: Create navigation menus by going to "Appearance" > "Menus." Add pages, categories, and custom links to create a menu structure that enhances user experience.
3. Installing Plugins: Plugins are extensions that add extra features and functionality to your website. Explore the "Plugins" section in your dashboard to find and install plugins that suit your needs, such as contact forms, social media integrations, SEO optimization, and more.
4. Adding Media: Enhance your content by incorporating images, videos, and audio files. Use the "Media" section to upload and manage your media files, and then insert them into your pages and posts.

5. Enhancing SEO: Improve your website's visibility in search engine results by optimizing it for SEO. Install an SEO plugin (e.g., Yoast SEO) to help you optimize your pages, posts, meta tags, and more.

Getting started with WordPress is an exciting journey that opens up endless possibilities for creating and managing a dynamic website. By choosing a reliable hosting provider, registering a domain name, installing WordPress, configuring basic settings, selecting a theme, and adding content and functionality, you'll be well on your way to building a professional and engaging website. Remember to explore the extensive WordPress community and resources for further assistance and inspiration. Embrace the flexibility and simplicity of WordPress to unleash your creativity and establish a strong online presence.

Chapter 2: Installing WordPress on Your Hosting Server

WordPress is a popular content management system (CMS) that allows you to create and manage websites with ease. To get started with WordPress, you need to install it on your hosting server. This process may seem daunting if you're new to web development, but it can be straightforward with the right guidance. In this guide, we will walk you through the step-by-step process of installing WordPress on your hosting server, enabling you to launch your website quickly and efficiently.

Step 1: Preparing for Installation

Before installing WordPress, you'll need to complete a few preparatory steps:

1. Choose a Hosting Provider: Select a hosting provider that meets your requirements in terms of reliability, performance, scalability, and customer support. Popular hosting providers include Bluehost, SiteGround, and DreamHost.
2. Domain Name: If you haven't already registered a domain name, do so before proceeding. A domain name is your website's address on the internet (e.g., www.yourwebsite.com).
3. Obtain Hosting Account Details: Once you've signed up with a hosting provider, you'll receive your hosting account details, including the nameservers, FTP credentials, and database information. Keep this information handy as you'll need it during the installation process.

Step 2: Creating a Database

WordPress requires a database to store your website's content and settings. Follow these steps to create a database:

1. Log in to your hosting control panel or dashboard. This interface may vary depending on your hosting provider.
2. Look for the "Databases" or "Database Management" section. Within that section, find the option to create a new database.
3. Provide a name for your database. Make it descriptive but easy to remember.
4. Create a username and password for the database. Ensure you choose a strong password for security purposes.
5. Add the database user to the database and grant it all privileges.
6. Take note of the database name, username, and password as you'll need them during the WordPress installation process.

Step 3: Downloading WordPress

To install WordPress, you need to download the WordPress software. Follow these steps:

1. Visit the official WordPress website at wordpress.org.
2. Click on the "Get WordPress" or "Download WordPress" button.
3. The latest version of WordPress will start downloading as a ZIP file.
4. Save the ZIP file to a location on your computer for easy access.

Step 4: Uploading WordPress to Your Server

To upload the WordPress files to your hosting server, follow these instructions:

1. Extract the contents of the WordPress ZIP file you downloaded in the previous step.
2. Connect to your hosting server using an FTP client. Popular FTP clients include FileZilla, Cyberduck, and WinSCP.
3. Enter your FTP credentials (FTP host, username, password, and port) in the FTP client to establish a connection.
4. Once connected, navigate to the root directory of your hosting server. This directory is usually named "public_html" or "www."
5. Upload all the extracted WordPress files to the root directory. This process may take a few minutes depending on the size of the files.
6. Once the upload is complete, you should see the WordPress files in the root directory of your hosting server.

Step 5: Configuring WordPress

Now that you have uploaded the WordPress files to your server, it's time to configure WordPress for your website:

1. Open a web browser and enter your website's URL (e.g., www.yourwebsite.com). You will be redirected to the WordPress installation page.
2. Select your preferred language for the WordPress installation and click on the "Continue" button.

3. On the next page, you will see a message stating that WordPress needs some information to proceed with the installation. Click on the "Let's go!" button.
4. Enter the database details you created in Step 2: the database name, username, password, and host. The host is usually "localhost" unless provided otherwise by your hosting provider.
5. Leave the table prefix as the default value unless you have a specific reason to change it.
6. Click on the "Submit" button to proceed.
7. WordPress will now check the database connection and verify the information provided. If successful, you will see a success message. Click on the "Run the installation" button.
8. On the next page, enter your website's title, username, password, and email address. Choose a strong password for the admin account.
9. After filling in the necessary details, click on the "Install WordPress" button.
10. WordPress will now install and set up your website. Once the installation is complete, you will see a success message.
11. Click on the "Log In" button to access your WordPress dashboard.

Step 6: Logging into Your WordPress Dashboard

To log into your WordPress dashboard, follow these steps:

1. Enter your website's URL in a web browser (e.g., www.yourwebsite.com).
2. Append "/wp-admin" to the URL (e.g., www.yourwebsite.com/wp-admin).
3. You will be redirected to the WordPress login page.

4. Enter the username and password you set during the installation process.
5. Click on the "Log In" button.

Congratulations! You have successfully installed WordPress on your hosting server and logged into your WordPress dashboard.

Installing WordPress on your hosting server is the first step toward building a successful website. By following the steps outlined in this guide, you can install WordPress with ease and begin customizing your website to suit your needs. Remember to keep your hosting account details, database information, and WordPress login credentials in a safe place for future reference. With WordPress installed, you are now ready to explore the vast array of themes, plugins, and customization options to create a unique and engaging website.

2.1 Exploring Themes and Customizing Your Site

One of the greatest advantages of using WordPress is the ability to customize your website's appearance and functionality through themes. Themes are pre-designed templates that determine the layout, design, and overall look of your website. By exploring different themes and customizing them to align with your brand or personal style, you can create a unique and visually appealing website. In this guide, we will explore how to find and install themes, as well as the various customization options available in WordPress.

Step 1: Finding and Installing Themes

WordPress offers a vast collection of themes that cater to different industries, styles, and purposes. Here's how you can find and install themes for your website:

1. Accessing the Theme Directory: From your WordPress dashboard, navigate to "Appearance" > "Themes." You will be directed to the Themes page, where you can explore available themes.
2. Featured Themes: WordPress showcases a selection of featured themes on the Themes page. Browse through these themes to see if any align with your website's vision.
3. Popular Themes: In addition to featured themes, you can also explore popular themes that have gained popularity among WordPress users. These themes are often well-designed and regularly updated.
4. Filtering and Searching: Use the filtering and search options to narrow down the themes based on specific criteria such as layout, color scheme, industry, or functionality. This helps you find themes that align closely with your website's requirements.
5. Previewing Themes: Before installing a theme, take advantage of the live preview feature. This allows you to see how your website would look with the theme without committing to it. Pay attention to the overall design, layout, typography, and navigation.
6. Installing Themes: Once you've found a theme you like, click on the "Install" button to add it to your WordPress installation. After installation, activate the theme to make it your website's active theme.

Step 2: Customizing Your Theme

After installing a theme, you can customize it to suit your preferences and make it unique. Here are the main customization options available in WordPress:

1. Customizer: The WordPress Customizer is a powerful tool that allows you to customize various aspects of your theme. To access the Customizer, go to "Appearance" > "Customize" in your WordPress dashboard. Here, you can modify settings such as site identity (logo, site title, tagline), colors, typography, header and footer layout, menus, widgets, and more. Each theme may have different customization options, so explore the available options specific to your chosen theme.

2. Widgets: Widgets are small content blocks that can be added to different sections of your website, such as sidebars, footers, or specific widgetized areas. To add widgets, go to "Appearance" > "Widgets" in your WordPress dashboard. Drag and drop widgets to the desired widget areas and configure their settings. Common widgets include a search bar, recent posts, categories, social media icons, and custom HTML.

3. Menus: WordPress allows you to create custom menus for navigation purposes. To create or edit menus, go to "Appearance" > "Menus" in your WordPress dashboard. Create a new menu, add menu items (pages, categories, custom links), and arrange their order. You can also create submenus for dropdown navigation.

4. Page Templates: Some themes offer different page templates that allow you to showcase your content in various formats. For example, you might have a template for a portfolio, a blog page, a full-width page, or a landing page. When creating or editing a

page, you can select the desired template from the "Page Attributes" section.

5. Custom CSS: If you have coding knowledge or want to make advanced design changes, you can add custom CSS to override the theme's default styles. This allows you to fine-tune the appearance of specific elements on your website. Use the "Additional CSS" option in the Customizer or consider using a custom CSS plugin for this purpose.

Step 3: Plugins for Enhanced Customization

To further enhance the customization options and functionality of your website, you can leverage WordPress plugins. Plugins are extensions that add specific features or capabilities to your site. Here are some popular plugins that can enhance customization:

1. Page Builder Plugins: Page builder plugins, such as Elementor, Divi Builder, or Beaver Builder, provide drag-and-drop interfaces to build custom layouts for your pages. These plugins offer a wide range of pre-designed elements and templates for easy customization.
2. Custom Fields Plugins: Custom fields plugins, such as Advanced Custom Fields, allow you to add additional fields to your posts, pages, or custom post types. This enables you to collect and display specific information beyond the default content fields.
3. Slider Plugins: Slider plugins, like Slider Revolution or MetaSlider, enable you to create dynamic and interactive image or content sliders for your website's homepage or other pages. This adds visual appeal and engages visitors.

4. Social Media Plugins: Social media plugins, such as ShareThis or Social Icons, allow you to integrate social media sharing buttons, follow buttons, or social media feeds into your website. This enhances your social media presence and encourages social sharing.
5. Contact Form Plugins: Contact form plugins, such as Contact Form 7 or WPForms, enable you to create and customize contact forms for your website. These plugins provide various form fields, styling options, and customization settings.

Exploring themes and customizing your site is an exciting process that allows you to transform a standard WordPress installation into a unique and visually appealing website. By finding and installing themes that resonate with your brand or style, and leveraging the customization options available in WordPress, you can create a website that reflects your vision and engages your audience. Remember to take advantage of the WordPress Customizer, widgets, menus, and plugins to enhance the customization process further. Regularly review and update your website's design to ensure it remains fresh, modern, and aligned with your evolving goals and objectives.

2.2 Creating and Managing User Accounts

WordPress allows you to create and manage user accounts, enabling multiple individuals to contribute to your website's content and functionality. User accounts provide varying levels of access and permissions, ensuring that each user can perform their designated tasks without compromising the overall security of the site. In this guide, we will explore the process of creating and managing user accounts in WordPress, including different user roles and their capabilities.

Step 1: Understanding User Roles

WordPress offers several predefined user roles, each with its own set of capabilities and permissions. Here are the primary user roles and their characteristics:

1. Administrator: Administrators have full control over the WordPress website. They can create and manage other user accounts, install plugins and themes, edit all content, modify settings, and perform any administrative task.
2. Editor: Editors have control over content management. They can create, edit, publish, and delete their own posts, as well as manage posts created by other users. However, they cannot modify themes, plugins, or other website settings.
3. Author: Authors can create, edit, publish, and delete their own posts. They have limited control over content management and cannot modify posts created by other users or access website settings.
4. Contributor: Contributors can create and edit their own posts, but they cannot publish them. Instead, their posts need to be reviewed and published by an Editor or Administrator. Contributors do not have access to other users' posts or website settings.
5. Subscriber: Subscribers have the most limited role. They can only manage their profile, leave comments on posts, and view restricted content. Subscribers cannot create or modify any content on the website.

Step 2: Creating User Accounts

To create user accounts in WordPress, follow these steps:

1. Log in to your WordPress dashboard using your Administrator account.
2. Navigate to "Users" > "Add New" in the WordPress dashboard.
3. Fill in the required fields for the new user, including username, email address, first name, last name, and password. Ensure that you choose a strong password for security purposes.
4. Assign a user role to the new user by selecting the appropriate role from the "Role" dropdown menu. Choose a role that aligns with the user's responsibilities and permissions.
5. Optionally, you can send the user an email notification with their login credentials by checking the "Send User Notification" box.
6. Click on the "Add New User" button to create the account.
7. The new user account will now be listed in the Users section of your WordPress dashboard.

Step 3: Managing User Accounts

WordPress provides various options for managing user accounts. Here are some common management tasks:

1. Editing User Accounts: To modify user account details, such as username, email address, or user role, follow these steps:

- Go to "Users" > "All Users" in your WordPress dashboard.
- Locate the user account you want to edit and hover over their username.
- Click on the "Edit" link to access the user's profile.
- Make the necessary changes and click on the "Update User" button to save the changes.

2. Deleting User Accounts: To remove a user account from your WordPress site, follow these steps:

- Go to "Users" > "All Users" in your WordPress dashboard.
- Locate the user account you want to delete and hover over their username.
- Click on the "Delete" link.
- You will be prompted to confirm the deletion. Choose the appropriate option based on whether you want to delete the user's content or reassign it to another user.
- Click on the "Confirm Deletion" button to delete the user account.

3. Password Reset: If a user forgets their password, WordPress provides a password reset option. To initiate a password reset, follow these steps:

- In the WordPress login screen, click on the "Lost your password?" link.
- Enter the username or email address associated with the user account.

- Click on the "Get New Password" button.
- An email will be sent to the user's registered email address with instructions on how to reset their password.

User Permissions and Access: WordPress allows you to modify user permissions and restrict access to certain areas of your website using plugins or custom code. This can be useful when you want to grant additional capabilities to specific user roles or limit access to sensitive information.

Creating and managing user accounts in WordPress is crucial for delegating responsibilities and ensuring the smooth operation of your website. By understanding the different user roles and their capabilities, you can assign appropriate permissions to each user. Additionally, knowing how to create, edit, and delete user accounts gives you control over who can contribute to your website. Regularly review and update user accounts to maintain a secure and organized user management system. With WordPress's user management features, you can effectively collaborate with others and streamline the content creation process.

2.3 Building Your Website's Foundation

Building a solid foundation for your website is essential for its long-term success. The foundation includes crucial elements such as choosing a domain name, selecting a reliable hosting provider, and configuring essential settings in WordPress. In this guide, we will explore the key steps involved in building your website's foundation, ensuring a strong and stable platform for your online presence.

Step 1: Choosing a Domain Name

A domain name is the unique web address that visitors will use to access your website. Here are some tips for choosing an effective domain name:

1. Reflect Your Brand: Select a domain name that aligns with your brand identity or website's purpose. It should be memorable and easily associated with your business or content.
2. Keep it Simple: Opt for a domain name that is easy to spell and pronounce. Avoid using complex or ambiguous words that might confuse visitors.
3. Use Keywords: If relevant, incorporate keywords related to your industry or niche in your domain name. This can help with search engine optimization (SEO) and make your website more discoverable.
4. Consider Extensions: Choose a domain extension that suits your website's purpose. Common extensions include .com, .org, and .net. If targeting a specific country, consider using a country-specific extension like .co.uk or .ca.
5. Research Availability: Use domain registration platforms to check the availability of your desired domain name. If your first choice is taken, consider alternatives or variations that are still relevant and accessible.

Step 2: Selecting a Hosting Provider

1. A hosting provider is responsible for storing your website's files and making them accessible to visitors. When selecting a hosting provider, consider the following factors:
2. Reliability and Uptime: Choose a hosting provider with a reputation for reliability and minimal downtime. Your website should be accessible to visitors at all times.
3. Speed and Performance: Look for hosting providers that offer fast loading times and optimal performance. A slow website can negatively impact user experience and SEO rankings.
4. Scalability: Consider the scalability options offered by the hosting provider. As your website grows, you may need additional resources or the ability to upgrade your hosting plan.
5. Customer Support: Ensure that the hosting provider offers reliable customer support that is easily accessible in case of technical issues or questions.
6. Pricing: Compare pricing plans and consider your budget while choosing a hosting provider. Balance cost with the features and services provided.

Step 3: Installing WordPress

WordPress is a user-friendly and versatile content management system (CMS) that powers millions of websites. Installing WordPress on your hosting server is a straightforward process:

1. Access your hosting account's control panel (usually cPanel).
2. Look for the "Auto Installers" or "Website Builders" section and click on the WordPress icon.

3. Follow the on-screen instructions, providing the necessary information such as your domain name, desired username, and password.
4. Once the installation is complete, you will receive a confirmation message with your WordPress login credentials.
5. Access your WordPress dashboard by appending "/wp-admin" to your domain name (e.g., www.yourwebsite.com/wp-admin) and logging in using the provided credentials.

Step 4: Configuring Essential Settings in WordPress

After installing WordPress, there are several essential settings you should configure:

1. Permalinks: Go to "Settings" > "Permalinks" and choose a permalink structure that is SEO-friendly and reflects the structure of your website.
2. General Settings: Navigate to "Settings" > "General" and configure basic settings such as site title, tagline, timezone, and date format.
3. Reading Settings: Determine how your website's front page displays content by going to "Settings" > "Reading." Choose between displaying a static page or your latest blog posts.
4. Discussion Settings: Manage comments and discussion settings by going to "Settings" > "Discussion." Enable or disable comments, set moderation rules, and configure other comment-related options.
5. Media Settings: Determine the default size and settings for uploaded media files in "Settings" > "Media."
6. Privacy Policy: Create a privacy policy page to comply with data protection regulations. You can use plugins or write a custom page.

Building a strong foundation for your website sets the stage for its success. By carefully choosing a domain name, selecting a reliable hosting provider, and configuring essential settings in WordPress, you establish a solid platform for your online presence. Remember to choose a domain name that reflects your brand, select a hosting provider that offers reliability and performance, and configure essential WordPress settings to optimize your website's functionality. With a solid foundation in place, you can focus on creating compelling content, engaging your audience, and achieving your online goals.

Chapter 3: Planning Your Website's Structure and Layout

Planning the structure and layout of your website is crucial for creating a user-friendly and organized online experience. A well-thought-out structure ensures that visitors can navigate your website easily and find the information they need. Additionally, a visually appealing layout enhances the overall user experience and captures the attention of your audience. In this guide, we will explore the key steps involved in planning your website's structure and layout.

Step 1: Defining Your Goals and Target Audience

Before diving into the specifics of your website's structure and layout, it is essential to define your goals and identify your target audience. Ask yourself the following questions:

1. What is the purpose of your website? Is it to provide information, sell products or services, showcase a portfolio, or engage visitors in some other way?
2. What actions do you want visitors to take on your website? Do you want them to make a purchase, sign up for a newsletter, contact you, or explore your content?
3. Who is your target audience? Consider their demographics, interests, and preferences. Understanding your audience helps tailor your website's structure and layout to their needs.

Step 2: Outlining Your Website's Structure

A clear and logical website structure makes it easy for visitors to navigate and find the information they seek. Here are some guidelines for outlining your website's structure:

1. Create a Main Navigation Menu: Identify the main sections or pages that should be included in your website's navigation menu. Common sections may include Home, About Us, Products/Services, Blog, Contact, and any other relevant categories.
2. Establish Hierarchy: Organize your content hierarchically, ensuring that related pages or sections are grouped together logically. Use submenus or dropdowns in your navigation menu to accommodate deeper levels of content.
3. Plan for Scalability: Anticipate future growth and expansion of your website. Structure your website in a way that allows for the easy addition of new pages or sections without disrupting the overall organization.
4. Consider User Flow: Visualize how visitors will navigate through your website. Ensure that important pages are easily accessible and that visitors can intuitively move from one section to another.

Step 3: Designing Your Website's Layout

The layout of your website influences its visual appeal and usability. Consider the following aspects when designing your website's layout:

1. Responsive Design: With the increasing use of mobile devices, it is crucial to create a responsive layout that adapts to different screen sizes. Ensure that your website looks and functions well on desktops, laptops, tablets, and smartphones.
2. Content Placement: Strategically position your content to prioritize important information. Place key elements such as your logo, navigation menu, and call-to-action buttons prominently.
3. Readability and Typography: Choose fonts and font sizes that are easy to read. Ensure sufficient contrast between text and background colors. Use headings, subheadings, and paragraph breaks to enhance readability.
4. Visual Elements: Incorporate images, videos, and graphics that align with your brand and enhance the overall aesthetic appeal of your website. Use them thoughtfully to support your content.
5. White Space: Utilize white space (or negative space) effectively to give your website breathing room and improve visual clarity. Avoid cluttering your layout with excessive elements.
6. Consistency: Maintain consistency in design elements, such as color schemes, fonts, and button styles, throughout your website. Consistency creates a cohesive and professional look.

Step 4: Wireframing and Prototyping

Wireframing and prototyping allow you to visualize the structure and layout of your website before diving into the actual development. Use wireframing tools or design software to create a skeletal framework for your website. Consider the placement of different elements, navigation flow, and overall user experience. Prototyping tools can help simulate interactivity and test usability.

Planning the structure and layout of your website is a vital step in creating a user-friendly and visually appealing online presence. By defining your goals, understanding your target audience, outlining your website's structure, and designing an engaging layout, you can create a website that effectively communicates your message and engages your visitors. Remember to prioritize usability, responsiveness, and consistency throughout the planning process. With a well-planned structure and layout, you are on your way to building a successful and engaging website.

3.1 Creating Pages and Organizing Content

Creating pages and organizing content are fundamental tasks when building a website. Pages serve as the main building blocks where you present information, showcase products or services, and engage with your audience. Organizing content effectively ensures that visitors can easily find what they're looking for, enhancing their overall user experience. In this guide, we will explore the key steps involved in creating pages and organizing content on your website.

Step 1: Planning Your Pages

Before creating individual pages, it's essential to plan their purpose and structure. Consider the following guidelines:

1. Define Page Types: Identify the different types of pages your website will have. Common page types include Home, About Us, Services, Products, Blog, Contact, and any other relevant categories specific to your website's goals.

2. Establish Page Hierarchy: Determine the relationship between your pages and their hierarchical structure. Create a logical flow that guides visitors through your website, starting from the main navigation menu.
3. Consider User Intent: Put yourself in the shoes of your target audience and consider their needs and goals. Ensure that each page provides relevant information and addresses visitors' potential questions or concerns.
4. Set Clear Call-to-Actions: Determine the desired actions you want visitors to take on each page. Whether it's making a purchase, filling out a contact form, or subscribing to a newsletter, design your pages to encourage these actions.

Step 2: Creating Pages in WordPress

WordPress provides a user-friendly interface for creating and managing pages. Follow these steps to create pages on your WordPress website:

1. Log in to your WordPress dashboard using your Administrator account.
2. Navigate to "Pages" > "Add New" in the WordPress dashboard.
3. Enter a title for your page in the designated field. Consider using descriptive and concise titles that reflect the content of the page.
4. Add content to your page using the visual editor. Use headings, paragraphs, lists, and multimedia elements (such as images and videos) to present your information effectively.
5. Format your content using the formatting toolbar options, including font styles, alignments, and text formatting.

6. Customize your page's appearance by selecting a page template, if available. Page templates can provide predefined layouts and styling options for specific page types.
7. Preview your page to see how it will appear to visitors. Make any necessary adjustments to ensure proper formatting and readability.
8. When you're satisfied with the page, click on the "Publish" button to make it live on your website.
9. Repeat the above steps to create additional pages, following your planned structure and content organization.

Step 3: Organizing Content with Menus

Menus allow you to create navigation systems that guide visitors through your website. WordPress provides a built-in menu editor for organizing your pages and custom links. Follow these steps to create and manage menus:

1. Access the WordPress dashboard and navigate to "Appearance" > "Menus."
2. Create a new menu by entering a name for it and clicking the "Create Menu" button.
3. Add pages to your menu by selecting them from the list of available pages and clicking the "Add to Menu" button. Alternatively, you can add custom links by entering the URL and link text.
4. Arrange the order of your menu items by dragging and dropping them into the desired position.
5. Create submenus (dropdown menus) by indenting menu items beneath others. Drag a menu item slightly to the right to create a submenu under a parent item.

6. Customize your menu settings, such as the menu location, by selecting the appropriate options provided by your theme.
7. Save your menu once you're satisfied with its structure and content.
8. Assign the menu to a specific location on your website by selecting the desired location from the "Menu Settings" section.

Step 4: Utilizing Categories and Tags

Categories and tags are useful tools for organizing and categorizing your content, particularly if you have a blog or news section on your website. Here's how to effectively utilize categories and tags:

1. Categories: Categories provide a hierarchical structure for organizing your content. Create categories that align with the main topics or themes of your website. Assign relevant categories to each blog post or article to make it easier for visitors to navigate and explore related content.
2. Tags: Tags are used to further describe and classify your content. Unlike categories, tags are not hierarchical and can be more specific. Add tags to your blog posts or articles to create associations and enable visitors to discover related content through tag-based navigation.
3. Use a Consistent System: Develop a consistent system for assigning categories and tags. This ensures that your content remains organized and easy to browse. Avoid excessive tags or categories that may confuse visitors.
4. Display Categories and Tags: Depending on your website's design and theme, you can display categories and tags on individual blog

posts or create dedicated category and tag archive pages where visitors can browse content within specific categories or tags.

Creating pages and organizing content are essential tasks in building a well-structured and user-friendly website. By planning your pages, creating them in WordPress, and organizing your content through menus, categories, and tags, you can provide a seamless browsing experience for your visitors. Remember to align your page structure with your website's goals, optimize content organization for user intent, and utilize menus, categories, and tags effectively to enhance navigation and content discovery. With a thoughtful approach to creating and organizing your website's pages and content, you can deliver a compelling and engaging experience to your audience.

3.1 Creating Pages and Organizing Content

Creating pages and organizing content are fundamental tasks when building a website. Pages serve as the main building blocks where you present information, showcase products or services, and engage with your audience. Organizing content effectively ensures that visitors can easily find what they're looking for, enhancing their overall user experience. In this guide, we will explore the key steps involved in creating pages and organizing content on your website.

Step 1: Planning Your Pages

Before creating individual pages, it's essential to plan their purpose and structure. Consider the following guidelines:

1. Define Page Types: Identify the different types of pages your website will have. Common page types include Home, About Us, Services, Products, Blog, Contact, and any other relevant categories specific to your website's goals.
2. Establish Page Hierarchy: Determine the relationship between your pages and their hierarchical structure. Create a logical flow that guides visitors through your website, starting from the main navigation menu.
3. Consider User Intent: Put yourself in the shoes of your target audience and consider their needs and goals. Ensure that each page provides relevant information and addresses visitors' potential questions or concerns.
4. Set Clear Call-to-Actions: Determine the desired actions you want visitors to take on each page. Whether it's making a purchase, filling out a contact form, or subscribing to a newsletter, design your pages to encourage these actions.

Step 2: Creating Pages in WordPress

WordPress provides a user-friendly interface for creating and managing pages. Follow these steps to create pages on your WordPress website:

1. Log in to your WordPress dashboard using your Administrator account.
2. Navigate to "Pages" > "Add New" in the WordPress dashboard.
3. Enter a title for your page in the designated field. Consider using descriptive and concise titles that reflect the content of the page.
4. Add content to your page using the visual editor. Use headings, paragraphs, lists, and multimedia elements (such as images and videos) to present your information effectively.

5. Format your content using the formatting toolbar options, including font styles, alignments, and text formatting.
6. Customize your page's appearance by selecting a page template, if available. Page templates can provide predefined layouts and styling options for specific page types.
7. Preview your page to see how it will appear to visitors. Make any necessary adjustments to ensure proper formatting and readability.
8. When you're satisfied with the page, click on the "Publish" button to make it live on your website.
9. Repeat the above steps to create additional pages, following your planned structure and content organization.

Step 3: Organizing Content with Menus

Menus allow you to create navigation systems that guide visitors through your website. WordPress provides a built-in menu editor for organizing your pages and custom links. Follow these steps to create and manage menus:

1. Access the WordPress dashboard and navigate to "Appearance" > "Menus."
2. Create a new menu by entering a name for it and clicking the "Create Menu" button.
3. Add pages to your menu by selecting them from the list of available pages and clicking the "Add to Menu" button. Alternatively, you can add custom links by entering the URL and link text.
4. Arrange the order of your menu items by dragging and dropping them into the desired position.

5. Create submenus (dropdown menus) by indenting menu items beneath others. Drag a menu item slightly to the right to create a submenu under a parent item.
6. Customize your menu settings, such as the menu location, by selecting the appropriate options provided by your theme.
7. Save your menu once you're satisfied with its structure and content.
8. Assign the menu to a specific location on your website by selecting the desired location from the "Menu Settings" section.

Step 4: Utilizing Categories and Tags

Categories and tags are useful tools for organizing and categorizing your content, particularly if you have a blog or news section on your website. Here's how to effectively utilize categories and tags:

1. Categories: Categories provide a hierarchical structure for organizing your content. Create categories that align with the main topics or themes of your website. Assign relevant categories to each blog post or article to make it easier for visitors to navigate and explore related content.
2. Tags: Tags are used to further describe and classify your content. Unlike categories, tags are not hierarchical and can be more specific. Add tags to your blog posts or articles to create associations and enable visitors to discover related content through tag-based navigation.
3. Use a Consistent System: Develop a consistent system for assigning categories and tags. This ensures that your content remains organized and easy to browse. Avoid excessive tags or categories that may confuse visitors.

4. Display Categories and Tags: Depending on your website's design and theme, you can display categories and tags on individual blog posts or create dedicated category and tag archive pages where visitors can browse content within specific categories or tags.

Creating pages and organizing content are essential tasks in building a well-structured and user-friendly website. By planning your pages, creating them in WordPress, and organizing your content through menus, categories, and tags, you can provide a seamless browsing experience for your visitors. Remember to align your page structure with your website's goals, optimize content organization for user intent, and utilize menus, categories, and tags effectively to enhance navigation and content discovery. With a thoughtful approach to creating and organizing your website's pages and content, you can deliver a compelling and engaging experience to your audience.

3.2 Configuring Essential Plugins for Functionality

Plugins are a powerful feature of WordPress that allows you to extend the functionality of your website. With thousands of plugins available, it's important to choose and configure the essential ones that align with your website's goals and enhance its performance. In this guide, we will explore the key steps involved in configuring essential plugins for functionality on your WordPress website.

Step 1: Choosing Essential Plugins

Before diving into the configuration process, it's crucial to select the right plugins for your website. Consider the following factors when choosing essential plugins:

1. Identify Your Website's Needs: Determine the specific functionalities your website requires. This could include contact forms, search engine optimization (SEO), caching, security, social media integration, performance optimization, or e-commerce features, among others.
2. Read Reviews and Ratings: Look for plugins with positive reviews and high ratings. User feedback can provide valuable insights into the plugin's reliability, ease of use, and performance.
3. Check Compatibility and Updates: Ensure that the plugins you choose are compatible with your WordPress version and other plugins you're using. Regular updates indicate that the plugin is actively maintained and supports the latest WordPress standards.
4. Consider Plugin Support: Look for plugins that offer support options, such as documentation, forums, or direct contact with the developers. Reliable support can help troubleshoot issues and ensure a smooth user experience.

Step 2: Installing Essential Plugins

Once you've chosen the essential plugins for your website, follow these steps to install them:

1. Log in to your WordPress dashboard using your Administrator account.
2. Navigate to "Plugins" > "Add New" in the WordPress dashboard.

3. In the search bar, enter the name of the plugin you want to install or use relevant keywords to find suitable options.
4. Review the search results and click on the "Install Now" button next to the desired plugin.
5. After installation, click on the "Activate" button to activate the plugin on your website.
6. Repeat the above steps for each essential plugin you want to install.

Step 3: Configuring Essential Plugins

Configuring plugins is crucial to ensure they function optimally and align with your website's requirements. Although the configuration process varies depending on the plugin, here are some general guidelines:

1. Review Plugin Documentation: Read the plugin's documentation or visit its official website to understand its features, settings, and configuration options. The documentation often provides step-by-step instructions for optimal configuration.
2. Access Plugin Settings: Most plugins add a new menu item or settings section to your WordPress dashboard. Look for the plugin's name in the sidebar or top navigation menu and click on it to access its settings.
3. Configure General Settings: Adjust general settings according to your website's needs. For example, configure contact form fields, specify SEO meta tags, set caching options, or define security parameters.
4. Customize Appearance: If the plugin affects the visual elements of your website, customize its appearance to match your website's

design. For example, choose color schemes, button styles, or layout options.

5. Set Permissions and Access Levels: If the plugin involves user roles or permissions, configure them to control who can access certain features or perform specific actions on your website.

6. Test Functionality: After configuring the plugin, thoroughly test its functionality to ensure it works as intended. Check for any conflicts with other plugins or themes and address them accordingly.

7. Regularly Update And Maintain: Keep your essential plugins up to date by installing updates as they become available. Regular updates often include bug fixes, security patches, and new features.

Step 4: Plugin Optimization and Performance

To optimize your website's performance and ensure that essential plugins don't negatively impact its speed or functionality, consider the following tips:

1. Avoid Plugin Overload: While plugins can enhance functionality, installing too many can slow down your website and create conflicts. Only install the plugins you truly need and regularly review and remove any unused plugins.

2. Monitor Plugin Performance: Keep an eye on your website's performance using tools like Google PageSpeed Insights or GTmetrix. If a plugin significantly impacts performance, consider finding alternatives or optimizing its settings.

3. Use Plugin Performance Optimization Techniques: Some plugins offer optimization options, such as caching, lazy loading, or

minification. Configure these settings to reduce the load on your server and improve loading times.

4. Regularly Back up Your Website: Back up your website regularly to safeguard your data and ensure you can restore it in case of any issues caused by plugins or other factors.

Configuring essential plugins is crucial for enhancing the functionality and performance of your WordPress website. By carefully choosing the right plugins, installing them properly, and configuring their settings to align with your website's goals, you can optimize your website's functionality, improve user experience, and ensure smooth operation. Remember to regularly update and maintain your plugins, monitor performance, and optimize settings to avoid conflicts or performance issues. With well-configured essential plugins, your website will have the necessary features to engage your audience and achieve your online objectives.

3.3 Designing Your Website

Design plays a crucial role in creating an engaging and visually appealing website. A well-designed website not only attracts visitors but also enhances their user experience, effectively communicates your brand message, and drives desired actions. In this guide, we will explore the key steps involved in designing your website to create a visually stunning and user-friendly online presence.

Step 1: Define Your Brand Identity

Before diving into the visual design of your website, it's essential to define your brand identity. Consider the following aspects:

1. Brand Colors: Choose a color palette that reflects your brand's personality and resonates with your target audience. Use colors consistently throughout your website for a cohesive and memorable visual experience.
2. Typography: Select fonts that align with your brand's tone and style. Consider legibility, readability, and the overall aesthetics of the fonts. Use a limited number of fonts to maintain consistency and readability.
3. Logo and Visual Assets: If you have a logo or visual assets, incorporate them into your website design. Ensure that they are displayed prominently and contribute to the overall brand recognition.

Step 2: User-Centered Design

Designing your website with the user in mind is crucial for creating a positive user experience. Consider the following user-centered design principles:

1. Navigation: Create a clear and intuitive navigation structure that allows visitors to easily find the information they are looking for. Use descriptive labels and logical organization to guide users through your website.
2. Responsive Design: Ensure your website is responsive and optimized for different devices and screen sizes. Responsive

design ensures that your website adapts and provides an optimal viewing experience on mobile phones, tablets, and desktops.

3. Readability: Use appropriate font sizes, line spacing, and contrast to ensure the readability of your content. Break content into smaller paragraphs, use headings and subheadings, and utilize bullet points or numbered lists to improve scalability.

4. Visual Hierarchy: Establish a clear visual hierarchy by using different font sizes, colors, and spacing to highlight important elements. Guide visitors' attention to key messages, calls to action, and important information.

Step 3: Layout and Composition

The layout and composition of your website significantly impact its visual appeal and user experience. Consider the following guidelines:

1. Grid System: Use a grid-based layout to create a well-organized and balanced design. Grid systems help maintain consistency and alignment of elements throughout your website.

2. White Space: Embrace white space (also known as negative space) to give your website breathing room. White space helps improve readability, highlight important elements, and create a sense of elegance and simplicity.

3. Balance: Strive for visual balance in your design by distributing elements evenly. Balance can be achieved through symmetrical or asymmetrical arrangements, depending on your design goals.

4. Focal Points: Create focal points to draw attention to specific elements or messages. Use size, color, contrast, or positioning to make key elements stand out and guide users' attention.

Step 4: Visual Elements and Multimedia

Visual elements and multimedia enhance the aesthetics and engagement of your website. Consider the following:

1. Images and Graphics: Use high-quality images and graphics that are relevant to your content and brand. Optimize image sizes to ensure fast loading times. Consider using infographics or illustrations to present information in a visually appealing way.
2. Videos: Incorporate videos to showcase products, provide tutorials, or share engaging content. Ensure videos are optimized for web viewing and provide clear playback controls.
3. Icons and Buttons: Utilize icons and buttons to enhance the user interface and make actions more intuitive. Use recognizable and universally understood symbols to guide users and encourage interactions.
4. Consistency: Maintain consistency in the use of visual elements throughout your website. Consistent color schemes, typography, and visual styles contribute to a cohesive and professional appearance.

Step 5: User Testing and Iteration

After designing your website, it's essential to gather feedback from users and make iterative improvements. Conduct user testing to identify any usability issues, navigation challenges, or design flaws. Based on the feedback received, make necessary adjustments and refinements to enhance the overall user experience.

Designing your website involves careful consideration of your brand identity, user-centered design principles, layout and composition, visual elements, and user testing. By following these steps and paying attention to the aesthetics, functionality, and user experience, you can create a visually appealing and engaging website that effectively communicates your brand message and achieves your website's goals. Remember to continuously evaluate and refine your design to stay up to date with evolving trends and user expectations. With a well-designed website, you can captivate your audience, build trust, and drive desired actions on your online platform.

Chapter 4: Choosing the Right Theme for Your Business

Selecting the right theme is a critical decision when building a website for your business. A theme sets the overall design, layout, and functionality of your website, influencing its aesthetics and user experience. In this guide, we will explore the key considerations and steps involved in choosing the right theme that aligns with your business goals and represents your brand effectively.

Step 1: Identify Your Business Needs

Before diving into the vast selection of themes available, it's important to identify your business needs and website requirements. Consider the following factors:

1. Purpose and Goals: Clarify the purpose of your website and the goals you want to achieve. Determine whether your website will be primarily informational, e-commerce-focused, or a combination of both.
2. Target Audience: Understand your target audience's preferences, demographics, and expectations. Consider their browsing habits, device usage, and the type of content they are likely to engage with.
3. Brand Identity: Take into account your brand's visual identity, including colors, fonts, and overall style. Ensure the theme you choose complements and represents your brand effectively.
4. Functionality Requirements: Make a list of the specific functionalities your website needs. This could include features like

contact forms, portfolios, e-commerce capabilities, blog integration, or event calendars.

Step 2: Research and Explore Themes

Once you have a clear understanding of your business needs, it's time to research and explore themes. Consider the following steps:

1. Theme Marketplaces: Visit reputable theme marketplaces like ThemeForest, Elegant Themes, or WordPress.org's official theme directory. Browse through the available themes and use search filters to narrow down your options.
2. Theme Categories: Explore different theme categories that align with your business type or industry. Categories could include business, e-commerce, portfolio, blog, photography, or magazine-style themes.
3. Theme Demos: Preview theme demos to get a sense of their design, layout, and available features. Pay attention to the overall aesthetics, navigation, and user experience.
4. Ratings and Reviews: Check ratings and read reviews from other users to get insights into the quality, reliability, and support provided by the theme developers. Consider themes with positive reviews and high ratings.
5. Developer Reputation: Research the reputation of theme developers. Choose themes developed by reputable and experienced developers who provide regular updates and support.

Step 3: Evaluate Theme Features and Customization Options

When evaluating themes, consider the following features and customization options:

1. Responsiveness: Ensure the theme is responsive and mobile-friendly. A responsive design adapts to different screen sizes, providing an optimal user experience on mobile devices, tablets, and desktops.
2. Customization Options: Assess the level of customization offered by the theme. Look for themes that provide options to customize colors, fonts, layouts, and other visual elements without requiring extensive coding.
3. Page Builders Integration: Check if the theme is compatible with popular page builders like Elementor, Beaver Builder, or Divi. Page builders provide advanced customization options and allow you to create unique layouts without coding knowledge.
4. Plugin Compatibility: Consider the compatibility of the theme with essential plugins you may need for functionality, such as SEO, e-commerce, or contact forms. Ensure the theme supports popular plugins and won't create conflicts.
5. Demo Content: Some themes come with demo content that can be imported to kickstart your website. Evaluate the availability and quality of demo content to see if it aligns with your business needs.
6. Documentation and Support: Look for themes that provide comprehensive documentation and support options. Good documentation helps you understand and navigate the theme's features, while reliable support ensures assistance when needed.

Step 4: Consider Performance and Loading Speed

Website performance and loading speed are crucial for user satisfaction and search engine optimization. Consider the following factors related to performance:

1. Lightweight and Optimized Code: Choose themes that have clean, lightweight, and optimized code. Well-coded themes contribute to faster loading times and better overall performance.
2. Speed Tests: Test the demo of the theme using tools like Google PageSpeed Insights or GTmetrix to assess its loading speed. Themes with faster loading times provide a better user experience.
3. Optimization Features: Some themes include built-in optimization features like caching, minification, or lazy loading. These features can significantly improve your website's performance.

Step 5: Make an Informed Decision

After evaluating themes based on your business needs, customization options, features, performance, and support, it's time to make an informed decision. Consider the following:

1. Shortlist Themes: Narrow down your options to a shortlist of two or three themes that best align with your business requirements.
2. Compare Features: Create a comparison chart to evaluate the features, customization options, and performance of each shortlisted theme. This will help you make a more informed decision.

3. Demo Installation: If possible, install demos of the shortlisted themes on a test website to get a hands-on experience and assess their functionality.
4. Seek Expert Opinions: If you have access to web design professionals or developers, seek their opinions and advice on the shortlisted themes. Their expertise can provide valuable insights.
5. Finalize and Purchase: Once you have made your decision, proceed to purchase the theme from the official marketplace or theme developer's website.

Choosing the right theme for your business is a crucial step in creating a visually appealing and functional website. By identifying your business needs, researching themes, evaluating features and customization options, considering performance and support, and making an informed decision, you can select a theme that represents your brand effectively and enhances your website's user experience. Remember to regularly update your theme, customize it to match your brand identity, and seek professional assistance if needed. With the right theme, your business website will stand out, engage visitors, and contribute to your overall online success.

4.1 Customizing Your Website's Appearance

Customizing the appearance of your website is a crucial step in creating a unique and visually appealing online presence. With the flexibility and versatility of WordPress, you have a wide range of options to personalize your website's look and feel. In this guide, we will explore the key steps and considerations involved in customizing your website's appearance to align with your brand identity and engage your visitors effectively.

Step 1: Choose a Customizable Theme

The first step in customizing your website's appearance is selecting a theme that offers customization options. Look for themes that provide a built-in theme customizer or options panel, as these will give you more control over the design elements. Consider the following factors when choosing a customizable theme:

1. Design Flexibility: Ensure the theme allows you to customize various aspects of your website, such as colors, fonts, layout, and header/footer styles.
2. Visual Compatibility: Choose a theme that complements your brand identity and resonates with your target audience. Look for themes with a design aesthetic that aligns with your industry or business type.
3. Customization Options: Check if the theme offers a wide range of customization options, such as color schemes, font choices, widget areas, and page templates. The more options available, the more you can tailor the appearance to your liking.

Step 2: Access the Theme Customizer

Once you have installed and activated your chosen customizable theme, access the theme customizer. In the WordPress dashboard, navigate to "Appearance" and click on "Customize." The theme customizer provides a live preview of your website and allows you to make real-time changes to its appearance.

Step 3: Customize Colors and Typography

Colors and typography play a vital role in the visual appeal of your website. Use the following guidelines to customize these elements effectively:

1. Color Scheme: Select a color scheme that reflects your brand identity and enhances the overall aesthetics of your website. Experiment with different color combinations for elements like backgrounds, headers, text, links, and buttons.
2. Typography: Choose appropriate fonts that are easy to read and align with your brand's tone. Customize font styles for headings, paragraphs, and other text elements. Ensure consistent typography throughout your website for a cohesive look.

Step 4: Customize Layout and Structure

Customizing the layout and structure of your website allows you to create a unique user experience. Consider the following customization options:

1. Header and Footer: Customize the header and footer sections to include your logo, navigation menus, social media icons, and contact information. Tailor these elements to match your brand and make them easily accessible to visitors.
2. Page Layouts: Some themes offer different page layouts, such as full-width, boxed, or grid-based. Choose a layout that best showcases your content and suits your website's purpose.

3. Widget Areas: Take advantage of widget areas to add additional functionality and content blocks to your website. Customize widget placement and content to enhance the user experience and provide valuable information.
4. Menus and Navigation: Customize your website's menus and navigation to improve usability. Create clear and logical menu structures that allow visitors to navigate your website easily.

Step 5: Customize Images and Media

Images and media play a significant role in engaging visitors and conveying your message effectively. Consider the following customization options:

1. Logo and Branding: Upload your logo and customize its size, position, and appearance to reinforce your brand identity.
2. Featured Images: Customize the display of featured images on different pages or posts. Ensure the dimensions and aspect ratios are consistent for a polished look.
3. Image Galleries: Use the available customization options to style your image galleries. Experiment with grid layouts, lightbox effects, captions, and other settings to create visually appealing galleries.
4. Video and Audio Integration: Customize the display and placement of videos and audio files on your website. Consider embedding options, autoplay settings, and customization of player controls.

Step 6: Customize Page Templates and Post Formats

Take advantage of custom page templates and post formats to create diverse and engaging content. Consider the following customization options:

1. Page Templates: Customize the layout and design of specific pages, such as the homepage, contact page, or portfolio page. Use page templates to showcase different types of content effectively.
2. Post Formats: Customize the display and styling of different post formats, such as standard, gallery, video, audio, or quote formats. Use appropriate formatting options to enhance the visual appeal of each post.

Step 7: Test and Iterate

After customizing your website's appearance, it's crucial to test and iterate to ensure a seamless user experience. Conduct thorough testing on different devices and browsers to identify any layout issues or design inconsistencies. Gather feedback from users and make necessary adjustments to improve the overall appearance and usability of your website.

Customizing your website's appearance allows you to create a unique and visually appealing online presence that aligns with your brand identity. By selecting a customizable theme, accessing the theme customizer, customizing colors and typography, adjusting layout and structure, enhancing images and media, and utilizing page templates and post formats, you can create a website that captivates visitors and delivers your message effectively. Remember to regularly review and update your customization choices to stay current with evolving design trends and user preferences. With a well-customized website, you can establish a strong online presence and leave a lasting impression on your audience.

4.2 Incorporating Images and Media

Images and media are powerful elements that enhance the visual appeal and engagement of your website. They help convey your message, showcase your products or services, and create a memorable user experience. In this guide, we will explore the key considerations and steps involved in incorporating images and media effectively into your website.

Step 1: Image Selection and Optimization

When incorporating images into your website, it's important to choose high-quality visuals that align with your brand and content. Consider the following guidelines:

1. Relevance: Select images that are relevant to your website's purpose, content, and target audience. Ensure they enhance the overall message you want to convey.
2. Resolution and Quality: Use high-resolution images to ensure clarity and sharpness. Avoid using pixelated or stretched images that can negatively impact the user experience.
3. File Size Optimization: Optimize image file sizes without compromising quality. Large file sizes can slow down your

website's loading speed. Use image compression tools or plugins to reduce file sizes while maintaining visual quality.

4. Image Formats: Use appropriate image formats for different types of images. JPEG is suitable for photographs, while PNG is ideal for graphics with transparency. GIFs can be used for simple animations.

Step 2: Image Placement and Composition

How you place and compose your images significantly impacts their effectiveness. Consider the following aspects:

1. Placement: Strategically place images within your website's layout to draw attention and guide the user's eye. Consider using images as visual focal points, within content sections, or as background elements.
2. Composition: Pay attention to the composition of your images. Consider factors like framing, rule of thirds, balance, and visual hierarchy to create visually pleasing compositions.
3. Alt Text: Provide descriptive alt text for your images. Alt text is important for accessibility purposes and helps search engines understand the content of your images. Use relevant keywords but avoid keyword stuffing.

Step 3: Image Galleries and Sliders

Image galleries and sliders are effective ways to showcase multiple images in an organized and interactive manner. Consider the following:

1. Gallery Types: Choose the appropriate gallery type for your website. Options include grid-based galleries, masonry layouts, carousel sliders, or lightbox displays.
2. Image Captions: Add captions to your gallery images to provide context or additional information. Captions can enhance the user's understanding and engagement with the images.
3. Navigation and Controls: Ensure that users can easily navigate through your image galleries or sliders. Include intuitive navigation arrows, thumbnails, or pagination to allow users to explore the images effortlessly.

Step 4: Video Integration

Videos are dynamic and engaging media elements that can effectively convey information and capture the user's attention. Consider the following when incorporating videos:

1. Hosting Options: Decide whether to host your videos on your own server or use external video hostings platforms like YouTube or Vimeo. Hosting externally can save server resources and provide additional features like analytics and social sharing.
2. Video Formats: Use widely supported video formats like MP4, WebM, or Ogg to ensure compatibility across different browsers and devices.
3. Video Placement: Strategically place videos within your website's layout to maximize their impact. Consider using video as a header background, in product demonstrations, testimonials, or as educational content.
4. Autoplay and Controls: Choose whether your videos should autoplay or require user interaction to play. Include clear and

intuitive video controls, such as play/pause, volume, and fullscreen options.

Step 5: Audio Integration

Audio elements can create a more immersive and engaging user experience. Consider the following when incorporating audio:

1. Audio Formats: Use widely supported audio formats like MP3, WAV, or AAC to ensure compatibility across different browsers and devices.
2. Audio Player: Choose an audio player that matches your website's design and provides user-friendly controls. Include options for play/pause, volume control, and track selection if applicable.
3. Autoplay and Controls: Decide whether your audio should autoplay or require user interaction to play. Consider the user experience and potential disruptions autoplay audio may cause.

Step 6: Copyright and Legal Considerations

Ensure that you have the necessary rights and permissions for the images and media you incorporate into your website. Consider the following:

1. Original Content: Create and use original images, graphics, and media whenever possible to avoid copyright issues.

2. Stock Images: If you use stock images, ensure that you have proper licenses and comply with the terms and conditions of the image provider.
3. Creative Commons: If you use Creative Commons licensed images, familiarize yourself with the specific license terms and give appropriate attribution when required.
4. Media Release Forms: If you use images or media featuring individuals, obtain their consent and, if necessary, have them sign media release forms to use their likeness.

Incorporating images and media into your website adds visual appeal, engages visitors, and enhances the overall user experience. By carefully selecting and optimizing images, strategically placing them within your website's layout, utilizing image galleries and sliders, integrating videos and audio, and respecting copyright and legal considerations, you can create a visually captivating and immersive website. Remember to regularly review and update your images and media to keep your website fresh and engaging for your audience. With thoughtful incorporation of images and media, your website will stand out and leave a lasting impression on your visitors.

4.3 Enhancing Your Website's Functionality

Enhancing the functionality of your website is key to providing an exceptional user experience, achieving your website's goals, and staying competitive in the online space. Fortunately, WordPress offers a wide range of plugins and tools that can extend the capabilities of your website. In this guide, we will explore various ways to enhance your website's functionality and make it more efficient, interactive, and user-friendly.

Step 1: Understanding Your Website's Goals

Before diving into enhancing your website's functionality, it's important to have a clear understanding of your website's goals and objectives. Consider the following questions:

1. What is the primary purpose of your website? Is it to provide information, sell products/services, generate leads, or entertain?
2. What actions do you want visitors to take on your website? Do you want them to make a purchase, fill out a contact form, subscribe to a newsletter, or engage with your content?
3. What features or functionalities would help you achieve those goals? Consider features like e-commerce, appointment booking, event calendars, membership systems, or social media integration.
4. By clarifying your website's goals, you can focus on enhancing its functionality in ways that directly support those objectives.

Step 2: Choosing the Right Plugins

WordPress offers a vast ecosystem of plugins that can extend your website's functionality. When choosing plugins, consider the following factors:

1. Relevance: Select plugins that directly address the specific functionality you want to add to your website. Avoid installing unnecessary plugins that may slow down your site or introduce potential security risks.

2. Reviews and Ratings: Check the reviews and ratings of plugins before installing them. Look for plugins with positive reviews, frequent updates, and a large user base, as these are usually indicators of reliability and ongoing support.
3. Compatibility: Ensure that the plugins you choose are compatible with your WordPress version and other existing plugins. Incompatible plugins can cause conflicts and disrupt the functionality of your website.
4. Developer Support: Consider plugins that have active developer support and a dedicated community forum. This ensures that you can seek assistance if you encounter any issues or have questions about the plugin's functionality.

Step 3: Essential Functionality Enhancements

Here are some essential functionality enhancements you can consider for your website:

1. Search Engine Optimization (SEO): Install an SEO plugin to optimize your website for search engines. These plugins provide features such as XML sitemap generation, meta tag optimization, and content analysis to improve your website's visibility in search engine results.
2. Security: Enhance the security of your website by installing a security plugin that provides features like malware scanning, firewall protection, login security, and activity monitoring. Regularly update your plugins, themes, and WordPress core to address security vulnerabilities.
3. Website Performance: Use caching plugins to improve your website's loading speed. These plugins create static versions of

your pages, reducing server load and improving user experience. Additionally, optimize your images and minify your CSS and JavaScript files for faster loading times.

4. Contact Forms: Install a contact form plugin to enable visitors to easily contact you. Choose a plugin that offers customization options, spam protection, and integration with email marketing services if needed.

5. Social Media Integration: Enhance your website's social media presence by integrating social sharing buttons, follow buttons, and embedding social media feeds. This allows visitors to share your content and connect with your social media profiles.

Step 4: Advanced Functionality Enhancements

Depending on your website's goals and requirements, you may need more advanced functionality enhancements. Here are some examples:

1. E-commerce: If you want to sell products or services online, consider installing an e-commerce plugin like WooCommerce. This plugin provides features for product management, shopping cart functionality, payment gateways, and order tracking.

2. Membership Systems: If you want to offer exclusive content or create a membership-based website, choose a membership plugin that allows you to restrict content, manage user subscriptions, and offer different membership levels.

3. Appointment Booking: If you provide services that require scheduling appointments, install an appointment booking plugin. These plugins enable visitors to book appointments directly from your website, and they often include features like calendar management and email notifications.

4. Events Calendar: If you organize events or want to showcase upcoming events, install an events calendar plugin. These plugins allow you to create and manage events, display event details, and offer registration options.
5. Analytics and Tracking: Install an analytics plugin to track your website's performance and gain insights into visitor behavior. These plugins integrate with popular analytics services like Google Analytics and provide valuable data to help you make informed decisions.

Step 5: Testing and Optimization

After implementing new functionality enhancements, it's important to thoroughly test your website to ensure everything is working as intended. Pay attention to:

1. Functionality: Test all added features and functionalities to ensure they work correctly and provide a seamless user experience.
2. Compatibility: Check for any conflicts or compatibility issues between plugins or with your chosen theme. Resolve any conflicts to ensure the smooth operation of your website.
3. User Experience: Put yourself in the shoes of your website visitors and navigate through different pages and functionalities. Identify any usability issues or areas for improvement and make necessary adjustments.

Enhancing your website's functionality is crucial for achieving your website's goals, improving user experience, and staying competitive. By understanding your website's objectives, choosing the right plugins, implementing essential functionality enhancements, considering advanced features, and thoroughly testing your website, you can create a more efficient, interactive, and user-friendly online presence. Regularly review and optimize your website's functionality to ensure it aligns with your evolving needs and delivers an exceptional user experience. With a well-enhanced website, you can effectively engage your audience, drive conversions, and achieve your online goals.

Chapter 5: Enhancing Your Website's Functionality

Enhancing the functionality of your website is key to providing an exceptional user experience, achieving your website's goals, and staying competitive in the online space. Fortunately, WordPress offers a wide range of plugins and tools that can extend the capabilities of your website. In this guide, we will explore various ways to enhance your website's functionality and make it more efficient, interactive, and user-friendly.

Step 1: Understanding Your Website's Goals

Before diving into enhancing your website's functionality, it's important to have a clear understanding of your website's goals and objectives. Consider the following questions:

1. What is the primary purpose of your website? Is it to provide information, sell products/services, generate leads, or entertain?
2. What actions do you want visitors to take on your website? Do you want them to make a purchase, fill out a contact form, subscribe to a newsletter, or engage with your content?
3. What features or functionalities would help you achieve those goals? Consider features like e-commerce, appointment booking, event calendars, membership systems, or social media integration.
4. By clarifying your website's goals, you can focus on enhancing its functionality in ways that directly support those objectives.

Step 2: Choosing the Right Plugins

WordPress offers a vast ecosystem of plugins that can extend your website's functionality. When choosing plugins, consider the following factors:

1. Relevance: Select plugins that directly address the specific functionality you want to add to your website. Avoid installing unnecessary plugins that may slow down your site or introduce potential security risks.
2. Reviews and Ratings: Check the reviews and ratings of plugins before installing them. Look for plugins with positive reviews, frequent updates, and a large user base, as these are usually indicators of reliability and ongoing support.
3. Compatibility: Ensure that the plugins you choose are compatible with your WordPress version and other existing plugins. Incompatible plugins can cause conflicts and disrupt the functionality of your website.
4. Developer Support: Consider plugins that have active developer support and a dedicated community forum. This ensures that you can seek assistance if you encounter any issues or have questions about the plugin's functionality.

Step 3: Essential Functionality Enhancements

Here are some essential functionality enhancements you can consider for your website:

1. Search Engine Optimization (SEO): Install an SEO plugin to optimize your website for search engines. These plugins provide features such as XML sitemap generation, meta tag optimization, and content analysis to improve your website's visibility in search engine results.
2. Security: Enhance the security of your website by installing a security plugin that provides features like malware scanning, firewall protection, login security, and activity monitoring. Regularly update your plugins, themes, and WordPress core to address security vulnerabilities.
3. Website Performance: Use caching plugins to improve your website's loading speed. These plugins create static versions of your pages, reducing server load and improving user experience. Additionally, optimize your images and minify your CSS and JavaScript files for faster loading times.
4. Contact Forms: Install a contact form plugin to enable visitors to easily contact you. Choose a plugin that offers customization options, spam protection, and integration with email marketing services if needed.
5. Social Media Integration: Enhance your website's social media presence by integrating social sharing buttons, follow buttons, and embedding social media feeds. This allows visitors to share your content and connect with your social media profiles.

Step 4: Advanced Functionality Enhancements

Depending on your website's goals and requirements, you may need more advanced functionality enhancements. Here are some examples:

1. E-commerce: If you want to sell products or services online, consider installing an e-commerce plugin like WooCommerce. This plugin provides features for product management, shopping cart functionality, payment gateways, and order tracking.
2. Membership Systems: If you want to offer exclusive content or create a membership-based website, choose a membership plugin that allows you to restrict content, manage user subscriptions, and offer different membership levels.
3. Appointment Booking: If you provide services that require scheduling appointments, install an appointment booking plugin. These plugins enable visitors to book appointments directly from your website, and they often include features like calendar management and email notifications.
4. Events Calendar: If you organize events or want to showcase upcoming events, install an events calendar plugin. These plugins allow you to create and manage events, display event details, and offer registration options.
5. Analytics and Tracking: Install an analytics plugin to track your website's performance and gain insights into visitor behavior. These plugins integrate with popular analytics services like Google Analytics and provide valuable data to help you make informed decisions.

Step 5: Testing and Optimization

After implementing new functionality enhancements, it's important to thoroughly test your website to ensure everything is working as intended. Pay attention to:

1. Functionality: Test all added features and functionalities to ensure they work correctly and provide a seamless user experience.
2. Compatibility: Check for any conflicts or compatibility issues between plugins or with your chosen theme. Resolve any conflicts to ensure the smooth operation of your website.
3. User Experience: Put yourself in the shoes of your website visitors and navigate through different pages and functionalities. Identify any usability issues or areas for improvement and make necessary adjustments.

Enhancing your website's functionality is crucial for achieving your website's goals, improving user experience, and staying competitive. By understanding your website's objectives, choosing the right plugins, implementing essential functionality enhancements, considering advanced features, and thoroughly testing your website, you can create a more efficient, interactive, and user-friendly online presence. Regularly review and optimize your website's functionality to ensure it aligns with your evolving needs and delivers an exceptional user experience. With a well-enhanced website, you can effectively engage your audience, drive conversions, and achieve your online goals.

5.1 Optimizing Your Website for Search Engines

Search engine optimization (SEO) plays a crucial role in driving organic traffic to your website and improving its visibility in search engine results. By optimizing your website's structure, content, and technical aspects, you can enhance its relevance and authority in the eyes of search engines. In this guide, we will explore the key strategies and best practices for optimizing your website for search engines.

Step 1: Keyword Research

Keyword research is the foundation of any effective SEO strategy. It involves identifying the keywords and phrases that your target audience is using to search for information relevant to your website. Consider the following steps:

1. Brainstorming: Begin by brainstorming potential keywords related to your website's content, products, or services. Think about the terms your audience would use when searching for what you offer.
2. Keyword Tools: Utilize keyword research tools like Google Keyword Planner, SEMrush, or Ahrefs to expand your list of keywords. These tools provide insights into search volume, competition, and related keywords.
3. Relevance and Intent: Focus on selecting keywords that are highly relevant to your website and align with the user's search intent. Consider both broad keywords and long-tail keywords (more specific phrases) that have lower competition.

Step 2: On-Page Optimization

On-page optimization involves optimizing the elements within your website's pages to improve their visibility and relevance to search engines. Consider the following factors:

1. Title Tags: Craft unique and descriptive title tags for each page, incorporating relevant keywords. Keep them concise, around 60

characters, and ensure they accurately represent the content of the page.

2. Meta Descriptions: Write compelling meta descriptions that summarize the page's content and entice users to click. Include relevant keywords and keep the description under 160 characters.

3. Heading Tags: Use heading tags (H1, H2, H3, etc.) to structure your content and highlight important sections. Include relevant keywords naturally in your headings to improve readability and SEO.

4. URL Structure: Optimize your URL structure to be concise, descriptive, and keyword-rich. Avoid using complex or irrelevant characters and include relevant keywords in the URL.

5. Content Optimization: Create high-quality, unique, and engaging content that addresses the user's search intent. Incorporate relevant keywords naturally throughout the content, but avoid keyword stuffing.

6. Image Optimization: Optimize your images by using descriptive file names and adding alt text that includes relevant keywords. Compress images to improve the loading speed without compromising quality.

Step 3: Technical Optimization

Technical optimization focuses on the backend aspects of your website to ensure it is easily crawlable and indexable by search engines. Consider the following technical factors:

1. Website Speed: Improve your website's loading speed by optimizing image sizes, minimizing CSS and JavaScript files, and

using caching plugins. A faster website provides a better user experience and can positively impact your search rankings.

2. Mobile-Friendliness: Ensure your website is responsive and mobile-friendly. With the increasing number of users accessing the internet through mobile devices, search engines prioritize mobile-friendly websites in their rankings.

3. URL Structure: Use clean and user-friendly URLs that are easy to read and understand. Avoid dynamic URLs with parameters and consider using descriptive words instead.

4. XML Sitemap: Create and submit an XML sitemap to search engines. This helps search engines understand the structure of your website and index your pages more efficiently.

5. Robots.txt: Create a robots.txt file to guide search engine crawlers on which parts of your website to crawl and which to exclude. Ensure it is correctly configured to avoid accidentally blocking important pages.

6. Canonical Tags: Use canonical tags to indicate the preferred version of duplicate or similar content. This helps search engines understand which page to prioritize in search results.

Step 4: Link Building and Off-Page Optimization

Link building is an important aspect of SEO that involves acquiring high-quality backlinks from other reputable websites. Consider the following strategies:

1. Content Marketing: Create valuable and shareable content that naturally attracts links from other websites. This can include blog posts, infographics, videos, and guides that provide useful information to your target audience.

2. Guest Blogging: Contribute guest posts to authoritative websites in your industry. This allows you to showcase your expertise, gain exposure, and earn valuable backlinks.
3. Social Media Promotion: Share your content on social media platforms to increase visibility and encourage others to link to it. Engage with your audience and build relationships with influencers who can amplify your content.
4. Online Directories and Listings: Submit your website to relevant online directories and listings. This helps increase your online visibility and can result in valuable backlinks.
5. Influencer Outreach: Connect with influencers and thought leaders in your industry. Collaborate on content, interviews, or partnerships that can lead to link opportunities and increased exposure.

Step 5: Monitoring and Continuous Optimization

SEO is an ongoing process, and it's important to monitor your website's performance and make adjustments as needed. Consider the following:

1. Analytics: Set up Google Analytics or other website analytics tools to track your website's performance. Monitor metrics like organic traffic, bounce rate, time on page, and conversions to gain insights into user behavior.
2. Keyword Rankings: Regularly monitor your keyword rankings to see how your website is performing in search results. Identify opportunities to improve and optimize further.
3. User Experience: Continuously assess and improve the user experience of your website. Ensure it is easy to navigate, visually appealing and provides valuable content to visitors.

4. Algorithm Updates: Stay informed about search engine algorithm updates and SEO best practices. Search engines regularly refine their algorithms, and staying up-to-date helps you adapt and maintain your website's visibility.

Optimizing your website for search engines is essential for driving organic traffic and increasing your online visibility. By conducting thorough keyword research, implementing on-page and technical optimization techniques, engaging in link-building activities, and monitoring your website's performance, you can improve your search engine rankings and attract a larger audience. Remember, SEO is an ongoing process, so continuously optimize and adapt your website to stay ahead of the competition and provide the best user experience possible.

5.2 Implementing E-commerce Functionality

E-commerce functionality allows you to sell products or services online, opening up new opportunities for revenue generation and reaching a wider audience. WordPress offers a variety of plugins and tools that make it easy to set up and manage an e-commerce website. In this guide, we will explore the key steps and considerations for implementing e-commerce functionality on your WordPress website.

Step 1: Choosing the Right E-commerce Plugin

Selecting the right e-commerce plugin is crucial for building a successful online store. Consider the following factors when choosing an e-commerce plugin:

1. Features: Evaluate the features offered by different e-commerce plugins. Look for essential features such as product management, shopping cart functionality, secure payment gateways, inventory management, and order tracking.
2. Scalability: Consider the scalability of the plugin. Will it be able to handle your future growth and increase product inventory? Ensure that the plugin can accommodate your long-term business needs.
3. Integration: Check if the e-commerce plugin integrates seamlessly with other essential tools and services, such as payment gateways, shipping providers, and email marketing platforms. Integration with popular services like PayPal, Stripe, and Mailchimp can simplify your operations.
4. Customization: Look for a plugin that offers customization options to match your branding and design preferences. The ability to customize product pages, checkout processes, and email templates can enhance the user experience and strengthen your brand identity.
5. Support and Updates: Consider the level of support and frequency of updates provided by the plugin developer. Regular updates ensure compatibility with the latest WordPress version and address any security vulnerabilities.

Step 2: Setting Up Your Product Catalog

To start selling products or services, you need to create a well-organized and visually appealing product catalog. Follow these steps to set up your product catalog:

1. Product Categories and Attributes: Organize your products into categories and subcategories to help customers navigate your store.

Define attributes such as size, color, or material to provide detailed product information and facilitate filtering options.

2. Product Descriptions and Images: Write compelling and informative product descriptions that highlight the features, benefits, and unique selling points of each item. Use high-quality images that showcase the product from different angles to help customers make informed purchasing decisions.

3. Pricing and Inventory Management: Set prices for your products and manage inventory levels to prevent overselling. E-commerce plugins usually offer options for setting regular prices, sale prices, and stock management.

4. Product Variations: If you offer products with different variations, such as different sizes or colors, set up variations within your product catalog. This allows customers to select their preferred options and see the corresponding price and availability.

Step 3: Configuring Payment Gateways

Payment gateways are essential for securely processing online transactions. Most e-commerce plugins offer integration with popular payment gateways. Follow these steps to configure payment gateways:

1. Research Available Options: Research and select the payment gateways that best suit your business needs and target market. Consider factors such as transaction fees, security features, ease of use, and supported currencies.

2. Account Setup: Sign up for an account with the chosen payment gateway and complete the necessary verification and documentation.

3. Plugin Integration: Install and configure the payment gateway plugin on your WordPress website. Enter the required API credentials provided by the payment gateway to establish a connection.
4. Test Transactions: Perform test transactions to ensure that the payment gateway is functioning correctly. Test different payment methods, such as credit cards or digital wallets, to ensure a smooth checkout process for customers.

Step 4: Designing a User-Friendly Shopping Cart and Checkout Process

A user-friendly shopping cart and checkout process are vital for a positive user experience and increased conversions. Consider the following best practices:

1. Shopping Cart: Ensure that the shopping cart is easily accessible and visible throughout the website. Display relevant information such as product details, quantities, and total prices. Offer the option to edit or remove items from the cart.
2. Simplified Checkout: Minimize the number of steps required to complete the checkout process. Implement a streamlined, single-page checkout or a progress indicator that clearly shows the steps involved.
3. Guest Checkout Option: Provide a guest checkout option to allow customers to make purchases without creating an account. This reduces friction and increases the likelihood of conversions.
4. Security Measures: Implement SSL certificates to encrypt sensitive customer data and reassure them of the security of their

transactions. Display trust badges and security seals to further instill confidence in your customers.

Step 5: Shipping and Order Management

Efficient shipping and order management processes are crucial for smooth operations. Consider the following steps:

1. Shipping Methods and Rates: Set up shipping methods and rates based on your product dimensions, weight, and destination. Offer options such as standard shipping, expedited shipping, or free shipping for specific order thresholds.
2. Integration with Shipping Providers: Integrate your e-commerce plugin with shipping providers such as UPS, FedEx, or USPS to automatically calculate shipping costs, generate shipping labels, and provide tracking information to customers.
3. Order Management: Set up systems to manage and track orders effectively. This includes order notifications, order status updates, and the ability to view and process orders from a centralized dashboard.
4. Customer Communication: Automate order confirmation emails, shipping notifications, and delivery updates to keep customers informed about their orders. Provide customer support channels for inquiries or assistance related to orders.

Step 6: Security and Compliance

Maintaining the security and compliance of your e-commerce website is essential for protecting customer data and maintaining trust. Consider the following measures:

1. Secure Sockets Layer (SSL): Install an SSL certificate to encrypt sensitive customer information and secure online transactions. This ensures that customer data, including payment details, is transmitted securely.
2. PCI Compliance: Ensure that your e-commerce website is PCI (Payment Card Industry) compliant if you handle credit card transactions. PCI compliance helps safeguard customer cardholder data and prevents unauthorized access.
3. Regular Updates and Backups: Keep your e-commerce plugin, theme, and WordPress core up to date to address security vulnerabilities. Regularly back up your website to protect against data loss.
4. Privacy Policy and Terms of Service: Display a clear and comprehensive privacy policy and terms of service on your website. These documents outline how customer data is collected, stored, and used, and they establish transparency and trust.

Implementing e-commerce functionality on your WordPress website opens up new opportunities for online business growth. By choosing the right e-commerce plugin, setting up a comprehensive product catalog, configuring secure payment gateways, designing a user-friendly shopping cart and checkout process, managing shipping and orders efficiently, and ensuring security and compliance, you can create a seamless and secure online shopping experience for your customers. Regularly evaluate and optimize your e-commerce processes to provide a satisfying user experience, drive conversions, and grow your online business.

5.3 Maintaining and Securing Your Website

Maintaining and securing your website is crucial for its performance, reliability, and protection against cyber threats. Regular maintenance ensures that your website remains up-to-date, optimized, and free from technical issues while implementing robust security measures to safeguard sensitive data and prevent unauthorized access. In this guide, we will explore the key steps and best practices for maintaining and securing your website effectively.

Part 1: Website Maintenance

1. Regular Updates:

Keeping your website, including the core WordPress software, themes, and plugins, up to date is essential for performance, compatibility, and security. Regularly check for updates and apply them promptly. Enable automatic updates where possible for convenience and timely patching.

2. Backup Strategy:

Implement a robust backup strategy to protect your website data in case of data loss, hacking, or server failure. Schedule regular backups of your website files and database, and store them securely in offsite locations or cloud storage. Test your backup restoration process periodically to ensure its reliability.

3. Database Optimization:

Optimize your website's database to improve its performance and efficiency. Use plugins or manual techniques to remove unnecessary data, clean up spam comments, and optimize database tables. Regularly optimize your database to maintain its health and responsiveness.

4. Broken Links and 404 Errors:

Regularly scan your website for broken links and 404 errors. Broken links negatively impact user experience and search engine rankings. Use tools or plugins to identify broken links and fix them promptly by updating or redirecting them to relevant pages.

5. Performance Optimization:

Optimize your website for faster loading speed and better user experience. Use caching plugins, compress images, minify CSS and JavaScript files, and enable browser caching. Regularly monitor your website's performance using tools like Google PageSpeed Insights and make necessary optimizations.

6. User Experience and Design:

Regularly review and update your website's design, layout, and user experience. Ensure that your website is mobile-friendly, visually appealing, and easy to navigate. Update content, remove outdated information, and make improvements based on user feedback and analytics data.

Part 2: Website Security

1. Strong Passwords:

Use strong, unique passwords for all user accounts, including the administrator account. Avoid using easily guessable passwords and consider using password management tools to generate and securely store complex passwords.

2. User Roles and Permissions:

Assign appropriate user roles and permissions to ensure that only authorized individuals have access to sensitive areas of your website. Regularly review user accounts and revoke access for inactive or unnecessary accounts.

3. Secure Hosting Environment:

Choose a reputable and secure hosting provider that offers advanced security features, including firewalls, intrusion detection systems, and regular server updates. Select a hosting plan that meets your website's needs and provides SSL certificates for secure data transmission.

4. SSL Encryption:

Enable SSL (Secure Sockets Layer) encryption on your website to encrypt sensitive data transmitted between your server and users' browsers. SSL certificates ensure secure connections and build trust with your visitors. Consider using HTTPS for your entire website.

5. WordPress Security Plugins:

Install and configure reliable security plugins to enhance your website's security. These plugins can provide features such as malware scanning, login protection, IP blocking, two-factor authentication, and firewall protection.

6. Vulnerability Monitoring:

Regularly scan your website for vulnerabilities using security plugins or online vulnerability scanners. Stay informed about the latest security threats and patch vulnerabilities promptly to prevent potential attacks.

7. *Malware Monitoring and Removal:*

Implement regular malware scans to detect and remove any malicious code or malware on your website. Use security plugins or online scanning tools to identify and clean infected files. Keep your plugins and themes updated to prevent vulnerabilities that could be exploited by hackers.

8. *Secure File Permissions:*

Set appropriate file permissions on your website's files and directories to prevent unauthorized access. Restrict write access to sensitive files and directories to minimize the risk of file modifications or unauthorized uploads.

9. *Regular Audits and Monitoring:*

Regularly audit your website's security settings, user accounts, and activity logs. Monitor your website for suspicious activities, such as multiple failed login attempts or unauthorized file modifications. Set up security notifications or alerts to be notified of potential security breaches.

Maintaining and securing your website is an ongoing process that requires proactive measures and regular attention. By following best practices for website maintenance, including regular updates, backups, performance optimization, and user experience improvements, you can ensure that your website remains in optimal condition. Implementing robust security measures, such as strong passwords, secure hosting, SSL encryption, security plugins, and vulnerability monitoring, helps protect your website from cyber threats. Regular audits and monitoring further enhance your website's security and enable quick responses to any security incidents. By prioritizing website maintenance and security, you can safeguard your website's integrity, protect sensitive data, and provide a secure experience for your users.

Chapter 6: Backing Up and Restoring Your WordPress Site

Backing up your WordPress site is crucial to protect your website data and ensure that you can recover your website in the event of data loss, hacking, or server failure. Regularly creating backups and understanding the process of restoring your site are essential steps in maintaining the integrity and availability of your WordPress website. In this guide, we will explore the key steps and best practices for backing up and restoring your WordPress site effectively.

Part 1: Backing Up Your WordPress Site

1. Determine Backup Frequency:

Decide how often you want to create backups based on the frequency of updates and changes to your website. Generally, it is recommended to perform backups at least once a week or more frequently for high-traffic or frequently updated sites.

2. Choose a Backup Method:

There are several backup methods available for WordPress sites. Consider the following options:

a. Manual Backups: Manually copy your website files and database using FTP (File Transfer Protocol) and phpMyAdmin. This method requires technical knowledge and is suitable for advanced users.
b. Backup Plugins: Install and configure a reliable backup plugin that automates the backup process. Popular backup plugins include UpdraftPlus, BackWPup, and Duplicator. These plugins offer various features such as scheduled backups, cloud storage integration, and incremental backups.
c. Managed Hosting Backups: Some managed hosting providers offer automated backup solutions as part of their services. Check if your hosting provider offers regular backups and understand their retention policies.

3. Select Backup Storage:

Choose a secure and reliable storage location for your backups. Options include:

1. Local Storage: Save backups on your local computer or an external hard drive. This option provides direct control over your backups but may have limited storage capacity.
2. Cloud Storage: Utilize cloud storage services such as Dropbox, Google Drive, or Amazon S3. Cloud storage offers scalability, redundancy, and accessibility from anywhere.
3. Remote Server: Upload backups to a remote server or FTP space provided by your hosting provider or a third-party service. This option ensures offsite storage and reduces the risk of data loss.

4. Configure Backup Settings:

If using a backup plugin, configure the settings according to your preferences. Specify backup frequency, storage location, retention period, and whether to include files, database, or both. Set up email notifications to receive backup status updates.

5. Test Backup Restoration:

Periodically test the backup restoration process to ensure that your backups are functioning correctly. Create a test environment or a subdomain where you can restore the backup and verify that your website functions properly.

Part 2: Restoring Your WordPress Site

1. Assess the Need for Restoration:

Determine the reason for restoration, such as a website crash, data loss, or security breach. Identify the appropriate backup version to restore based on the timing of the issue and the availability of backups.

2. Prepare the Restoration Environment:

Before initiating the restoration process, prepare the restoration environment:

a. Install a Fresh WordPress Installation: If your WordPress installation is corrupted or compromised, install a fresh copy of WordPress on your server or hosting account.
b. Clear Existing Website Data: Remove any existing files and databases from the restoration environment to avoid conflicts during the restoration process.

3. Restore Website Files:

Depending on your backup method, restore the website files using one of the following methods:

a. Manual Restoration: Upload the backup files to the appropriate directories on your server using FTP or the file manager provided by your hosting control panel.
b. Backup Plugin Restoration: If using a backup plugin, follow the plugin's instructions to restore the files from the backup storage location.

4. Restore Database:

To restore the database, follow these steps:

a. Manual Restoration: Use phpMyAdmin or a similar tool provided by your hosting provider to import the database backup file. Create a new database, if required, and import the backup SQL file into it.

b. Backup Plugin Restoration: If using a backup plugin, follow the plugin's instructions to restore the database from the backup storage location.

5. Update Website URLs and Settings:

After restoring the files and database, update the website URLs and settings to match the original configuration. Update the WordPress site URL and any other relevant settings in the WordPress dashboard.

6. Test and Verify the Restored Website:

Thoroughly test your restored website to ensure that all functionality, content, and design elements are working as expected. Check for broken links, missing images, and any other issues that may have occurred during the restoration process.

Backing up and restoring your WordPress site is a critical aspect of website management and security. By establishing a regular backup routine, selecting a suitable backup method, and storing backups securely, you can protect your website data and minimize the impact of potential incidents. Understanding the restoration process, preparing the restoration environment, and following the appropriate steps for file and database restoration enables you to recover your website effectively. Regularly test the restoration process to ensure the integrity of your backups. By implementing these best practices, you can confidently manage and safeguard your WordPress site and ensure its availability and reliability.

6.1 Updating WordPress, Themes, and Plugins

Regularly updating WordPress, themes, and plugins is crucial for the security, performance, and functionality of your website. Updates often include bug fixes, security patches, new features, and compatibility improvements. By keeping your website components up to date, you ensure that your site remains secure, optimized, and equipped with the latest features. In this guide, we will explore the importance of updating WordPress, themes, and plugins, as well as the best practices for performing updates effectively.

Part 1: Understanding the Importance of Updates

1. Security Enhancements:

One of the primary reasons to update WordPress, themes, and plugins is to address security vulnerabilities. Hackers constantly search for weaknesses in outdated software versions. By keeping everything up to date, you minimize the risk of security breaches and protect your website and user data.

2. Bug Fixes and Stability:

Updates often include bug fixes that address issues identified in previous versions. These bug fixes enhance the stability of your website, preventing crashes, errors, and unexpected behavior. Regular updates ensure that your website functions smoothly and provides a seamless user experience.

3. Compatibility Improvements:

As technology evolves, updates ensure that your website remains compatible with the latest browsers, devices, and web standards. Updates also address compatibility issues that may arise due to changes in WordPress core, themes, or plugins. By staying up to date, you ensure that your website functions optimally across various platforms.

4. Performance Optimization:

Updates often include performance optimizations that improve the speed and efficiency of your website. These optimizations can enhance page load times, reduce server resource usage, and improve overall website performance. Regular updates help you deliver a fast and responsive user experience.

Part 2: Best Practices for Updating WordPress, Themes, and Plugins

1. Backup Your Website:

Before performing any updates, create a backup of your website files and database. This serves as a safety net in case any issues arise during the update process. Ensure that your backup is stored securely and can be easily restored if needed.

2. Update WordPress Core:

Start by updating the WordPress core. When a new version is available, WordPress will display a notification in the dashboard. Click the Update button to initiate the update process. It is essential to keep the core up to date for security, stability, and new features.

3. Update Themes:

Next, update your WordPress themes. If you are using a free theme from the official WordPress theme repository, you can update it directly from the Themes section in the WordPress dashboard. For premium themes or custom themes, follow the instructions provided by the theme developer or use a theme update plugin if available.

4. Update Plugins:

After updating the core and themes, it's time to update your plugins. Similar to themes, you can update free plugins from the Plugins section in the WordPress dashboard. For premium or custom plugins, refer to the plugin documentation or developer's instructions for updating.

5. Update in a Staging Environment:

For complex websites or those with critical functionality, consider performing updates in a staging environment before applying them to the live site. A staging environment allows you to test updates and ensure compatibility and stability before making them live.

6. Test Your Website:

After updating WordPress, themes, and plugins, thoroughly test your website to ensure everything is functioning as expected. Check for any visual or functional issues, broken links, or compatibility problems. Test different areas of your website, including forms, navigation, and interactive elements.

7. Monitor for Compatibility Issues:

After updating, monitor your website for any compatibility issues that may arise. Sometimes conflicts between different themes, plugins, or WordPress versions can occur. Stay vigilant and address any compatibility issues promptly by seeking support from theme or plugin developers or by considering alternative solutions.

8. Remove Unnecessary Themes and Plugins:

Regularly review your installed themes and plugins and remove any that are no longer in use. Unnecessary themes and plugins can pose security risks if not updated regularly. Removing them reduces the attack surface and simplifies the update process.

Updating WordPress, themes, and plugins is a critical aspect of maintaining a secure, optimized, and fully functional website. By prioritizing updates, you ensure that your website remains protected against security threats, benefits from bug fixes and stability improvements, remains compatible with evolving technologies and delivers optimal performance. Following best practices, such as backing up your website, updating in a staging environment, and thorough testing, minimizes the risk of issues during the update process. Stay proactive in monitoring compatibility issues and removing unnecessary themes and plugins. By adhering to these practices, you can effectively manage updates and maintain a secure and reliable WordPress website.

6.2 Implementing Security Measures and Best Practices

In today's digital landscape, implementing robust security measures for your website is crucial to protect it against potential threats and ensure the safety of your data and users. By following security best practices and implementing appropriate security measures, you can minimize the risk of unauthorized access, data breaches, malware infections, and other security vulnerabilities. In this guide, we will explore essential security measures and best practices that you can implement to enhance the security of your website effectively.

1. **Strong Password Policies:**

Enforce strong password policies for all user accounts, including administrators, editors, and contributors. Encourage the use of long, complex passwords that include a combination of uppercase and lowercase letters, numbers, and special characters. Implementing a password strength meter can help users create stronger passwords.

2. Two-Factor Authentication (2FA):

Enable two-factor authentication for user logins to add an extra layer of security. 2FA requires users to provide a second form of authentication, such as a unique code sent to their mobile device, in addition to their username and password. This significantly reduces the risk of unauthorized access even if passwords are compromised.

3. Regular Updates:

Keep your website's core, themes, and plugins up to date. Regular updates often include security patches that address known vulnerabilities. Enable automatic updates whenever possible, but also regularly check for updates manually to ensure that all components are up to date.

4. Secure Hosting:

Choose a reputable and secure hosting provider that prioritizes website security. Look for hosting providers that offer SSL certificates, provide regular backups, use firewalls, and have robust security protocols in place. Consider managed WordPress hosting options that handle security updates and monitoring on your behalf.

5. Use Secure Sockets Layer (SSL) Encryption:

Implement SSL encryption on your website to secure data transmitted between your website and users' browsers. SSL certificates enable the HTTPS protocol, encrypting sensitive information such as login credentials, payment details, and personal data. This enhances user trust and protects against data interception.

6. Limit Login Attempts:

Install a plugin that limits the number of login attempts allowed within a specific timeframe. This helps protect against brute-force attacks where hackers attempt to guess passwords by repeatedly trying different combinations. Limiting login attempts prevents automated attacks and unauthorized access.

7. Secure User Roles and Permissions:

Regularly review and manage user roles and permissions. Only grant necessary privileges to users based on their responsibilities. Restrict administrative access to trusted individuals, and limit the number of accounts with administrative privileges.

8. Secure File Permissions:

Set appropriate file and directory permissions to prevent unauthorized access to sensitive files. Ensure that directories have read, write, and execute permissions set correctly, while files should have read and write permissions limited to necessary users.

9. Implement Web Application Firewall (WAF):

Consider using a web application firewall to monitor and filter incoming web traffic. A WAF helps detect and block malicious requests, such as SQL injections, cross-site scripting (XSS), and other common attack vectors. It acts as an additional layer of protection for your website.

10. Regular Backups:

Frequently back up your website's files and database to an external location or cloud storage. In case of a security incident or data loss, backups allow you to restore your website quickly. Automate the backup process to ensure regular and consistent backups.

11. Monitor Website Activity:

Implement a security monitoring system or use a security plugin that tracks and logs suspicious activities on your website. Monitor login attempts, file modifications, and any unusual behavior. Regularly review logs for any signs of security breaches or unauthorized access.

12. Remove Unused Themes and Plugins:

Remove any unused themes and plugins from your website. Unused themes and plugins can be potential security risks if not updated regularly. Reduce the attack surface by removing unnecessary components from your website.

13. Educate Users:

Provide security training and education to all users who have access to your website. Teach them about common security threats, best practices for password management, and how to identify and report suspicious activities. Regularly remind users about security protocols and the importance of maintaining a secure online environment.

Implementing security measures and best practices is essential for safeguarding your website from potential threats and maintaining the trust of your users. By following the recommended practices discussed in this guide, including enforcing strong passwords, enabling two-factor authentication, regularly updating your website, securing hosting, implementing SSL encryption, and monitoring website activity, you can significantly enhance your website's security. Remember that security is an ongoing process, and it requires continuous monitoring, updates, and adaptation to evolving threats. Stay informed about the latest security practices and be proactive in implementing necessary measures to protect your website and the sensitive data it holds.

6.3 Growing Your Website and Engaging Your Audience

Once you have set up your website and established a solid foundation, the next step is to focus on growing your website and engaging your audience effectively. Growing your website involves attracting more visitors, increasing user engagement, and expanding your online presence. By implementing various strategies and techniques, you can drive traffic to your website, retain visitors, and create a meaningful connection with your audience. In this guide, we will explore valuable insights and best practices for growing your website and engaging your audience successfully.

Part 1: Driving Traffic to Your Website

1. Search Engine Optimization (SEO):

Optimize your website for search engines to improve its visibility and organic rankings. Conduct keyword research, optimize meta tags, create quality content, and build high-quality backlinks. Focus on both on-page and off-page SEO techniques to increase your website's chances of ranking higher in search engine results.

2. Content Marketing:

Develop a content marketing strategy to attract and engage your target audience. Create high-quality, valuable content that is relevant to your audience's interests and needs. Publish blog posts, articles, videos, and other forms of content regularly. Promote your content through social media, email marketing, and guest blogging to expand your reach.

3. Social Media Marketing:

Utilize social media platforms to promote your website and engage with your audience. Create social media profiles on relevant platforms and share your content, interact with followers, and participate in industry-related conversations. Use social media advertising to target specific demographics and drive traffic to your website.

4. Email Marketing:

Build an email list and implement email marketing campaigns to stay connected with your audience. Offer incentives such as exclusive content or discounts to encourage visitors to subscribe. Send regular newsletters, updates, and personalized emails to provide value and drive traffic back to your website.

Part 2: Increasing User Engagement

1. Interactive Content:

Create interactive content to increase user engagement and encourage interaction. Incorporate elements such as quizzes, polls, surveys, and contests into your website. Interactive content not only captivates visitors but also encourages them to spend more time on your site and share their experiences.

2. User-Generated Content (UGC):

Encourage your audience to contribute to your website through user-generated content. Enable comments on blog posts, include social sharing buttons, and host discussions or forums where users can share their opinions and experiences. UGC fosters a sense of community and encourages visitors to become active participants.

3. Personalization:

Tailor your website's content and user experience to individual visitors based on their preferences and behaviors. Use personalization techniques to display relevant content, recommend related products or articles, and provide personalized recommendations. Personalization enhances user engagement by creating a more personalized and tailored experience.

4. Responsive Design:

Ensure that your website is responsive and optimized for various devices, including desktops, laptops, tablets, and smartphones. A mobile-friendly website provides a seamless user experience and allows visitors to engage with your content on any device. Responsive design also helps improve your website's search engine rankings.

Part 3: Expanding Your Online Presence

1. Guest Blogging:

Write guest posts for reputable websites in your industry to reach a wider audience and establish yourself as an authority. Include a bio or author's note that links back to your website, driving traffic and increasing your website's visibility.

2. Collaborations and Partnerships:

Collaborate with influencers, industry experts, or complementary businesses to expand your reach and tap into new audiences. Partner with relevant brands for co-marketing initiatives, cross-promotions, or joint events to increase your online presence and gain exposure to a wider audience.

3. Online Advertising:

Consider investing in online advertising to increase visibility and drive targeted traffic to your website. Utilize platforms such as Google Ads, social media ads, or display advertising to reach your desired audience and promote your website effectively.

4. Networking and Community Engagement:

Engage with your industry community by attending conferences, participating in webinars, joining relevant forums or online communities, and networking with peers. Building relationships within your industry can lead to collaborations, referrals, and opportunities to expand your online presence.

Growing your website and engaging your audience requires a combination of strategic planning, consistent effort, and a deep understanding of your target audience. By driving traffic to your website through SEO, content marketing, social media, and email marketing, you can attract a steady stream of visitors. Increasing user engagement through interactive content, user-generated content, personalization, and responsive design helps create a meaningful connection with your audience. Finally, expanding your online presence through guest blogging, collaborations, online advertising, and networking enables you to reach new audiences and further grow your website's visibility. Remember to continuously monitor and analyze your website's performance, adapt your strategies based on user feedback and industry trends, and stay committed to providing value and an exceptional user experience.

Chapter 7: Utilizing Social Media Integration

In today's digital age, social media has become an integral part of our daily lives, and it plays a crucial role in connecting people, sharing information, and promoting businesses. Integrating social media into your website can significantly enhance your online presence, engage your audience, and drive traffic to your website. By utilizing social media integration effectively, you can harness the power of social platforms to expand your reach, build brand awareness, and foster meaningful connections with your target audience. In this guide, we will explore the benefits of social media integration and provide insights on how to effectively implement it into your website.

Part 1: Benefits of Social Media Integration

1. Increased Website Traffic:

Social media integration enables you to drive more traffic to your website. By sharing your website's content, blog posts, product pages, or promotions on social media platforms, you can attract users who may not have discovered your website otherwise. Social media acts as a referral source, directing users to visit your website and explore further.

2. Enhanced User Engagement:

Integrating social media into your website allows users to engage with your content easily. They can like, comment, and share your website's content directly from your web pages. This interactive engagement promotes user participation and encourages them to share their experiences, opinions, and feedback.

3. Improved Brand Visibility:

Social media platforms have millions of active users, making them a prime opportunity to increase your brand's visibility. By integrating social media buttons or widgets into your website, visitors can easily follow and connect with your social media profiles, helping to build brand recognition and expand your online presence.

4. Social Proof and Trust:

When users see social media integrations on your website, such as social sharing buttons displaying high numbers of shares or followers, it enhances your credibility and establishes social proof. Social proof acts as a trust indicator, showing that others have found value in your content or products, thereby increasing trust and confidence in your brand.

Part 2: Effective Social Media Integration Techniques

1. Social Sharing Buttons:

Place social sharing buttons prominently on your website's pages to encourage visitors to share your content on their social media profiles. Ensure that the buttons are easily accessible and visually appealing.

Include popular social media platforms such as Facebook, Twitter, LinkedIn, Pinterest, and Instagram.

2. Social Media Feeds:

Display real-time social media feeds on your website to showcase your social media activity and encourage visitors to engage with your social profiles. Embed feeds from platforms such as Instagram, Twitter, or Facebook to display recent posts, hashtags, or user-generated content related to your brand.

3. Social Login:

Simplify the registration and login process for users by incorporating social login options. Allow users to sign up or log in using their social media accounts such as Facebook, Google, or Twitter. This eliminates the need for users to create new accounts, reducing friction and increasing conversion rates.

4. Social Media Integration with E-commerce:

If you have an e-commerce website, integrate social media features to enhance the shopping experience. Incorporate social sharing buttons on product pages to encourage users to share their favorite products on their social media profiles. Additionally, consider adding social proof elements like user-generated reviews or ratings.

5. Social Media Widgets and Plugins:

Utilize social media widgets or plugins to integrate your social media profiles directly into your website. These widgets can display your latest posts, follower counts, or social media activity, providing visitors with a glimpse into your social media presence and encouraging them to connect with you.

6. Social Media Commenting:

Replace or complement your website's native comment system with social media commenting options. Allowing users to comment using their social media profiles eliminates the need for a separate registration process and encourages more engagement as users can use their existing social media accounts to comment.

Part 3: Best Practices for Social Media Integration

1. Consistency in Branding:

Maintain consistent branding across your website and social media profiles. Use the same color schemes, logos, and messaging to reinforce brand recognition and ensure a seamless user experience as visitors navigate between your website and social media platforms.

2. Responsive Design:

Ensure that your social media integration is responsive and optimized for different devices. As users access your website from various devices, including smartphones and tablets, it is essential to provide a consistent and user-friendly experience regardless of the device they are using.

3. Regular Updates and Monitoring:

Regularly update your social media integrations to stay current with the latest features and functionality. Monitor the performance of your social media integration, track engagement metrics, and analyze user behavior to identify areas for improvement and optimize your integration strategies.

4. Privacy and Data Security:

When integrating social media, prioritize user privacy and data security. Ensure compliance with data protection regulations and clearly communicate your data collection and usage policies. Provide options for users to control their privacy settings and obtain consent before accessing their social media data.

Social media integration offers numerous benefits for your website, including increased traffic, enhanced user engagement, improved brand visibility, and social proof. By effectively implementing social media integration techniques such as social sharing buttons, social media feeds, social login, and social media widgets, you can leverage the power of social platforms to grow your online presence and foster meaningful connections with your audience. Remember to maintain consistent branding, prioritize responsive design, regularly update and monitor your integrations, and prioritize user privacy and data security. By harnessing the potential of social media integration, you can elevate your website's performance, engage your audience, and drive your online success.

7.1 Implementing Effective Content Marketing Strategies

Content marketing is a powerful strategy that involves creating and distributing valuable and relevant content to attract, engage, and retain a target audience. By implementing effective content marketing strategies, businesses can establish their expertise, build brand awareness, and drive profitable customer actions. In this guide, we will explore key insights and best practices for implementing content marketing strategies that can help businesses achieve their marketing goals.

Part 1: Understanding Content Marketing

1. Defining Your Objectives:

Before diving into content creation, clearly define your objectives for content marketing. Determine what you aim to achieve, such as increasing brand awareness, driving website traffic, generating leads, or nurturing customer relationships. Clear objectives will guide your content creation process and help measure the success of your efforts.

2. Understanding Your Target Audience:

Identify and understand your target audience's needs, preferences, and pain points. Conduct market research, analyze customer data, and create buyer personas to develop a deep understanding of your audience. This knowledge will guide your content creation process and ensure that your content resonates with your target audience.

3. Creating Valuable and Relevant Content:

Develop content that provides value to your audience. Create educational, informative, entertaining, or inspirational content that addresses their pain points, answers their questions, or offers solutions to their problems. Your content should be relevant to their interests and align with your brand's expertise and values.

Part 2: Content Creation and Distribution

1. Developing a Content Calendar:

Create a content calendar to plan and organize your content creation and distribution schedule. This helps ensure a consistent flow of content and allows you to align your content with relevant events, holidays, or industry trends. A content calendar also helps maintain a strategic approach to content creation and prevents haphazard publishing.

2. Diversifying Content Formats:

Explore various content formats to cater to different audience preferences. Create blog posts, articles, videos, infographics, podcasts, case studies, whitepapers, or interactive content. Diversifying your content formats adds variety, increases engagement, and allows you to repurpose content across different channels.

3. Optimizing Content for Search Engines:

Incorporate search engine optimization (SEO) techniques to increase your content's visibility in search engine results. Conduct keyword research, optimize your headlines, meta tags, and content structure, and build quality backlinks to improve your content's ranking. SEO helps attract organic traffic and ensures your content reaches the right audience.

4. Promoting Your Content:

Actively promote your content through various channels to maximize its reach. Utilize social media platforms, email marketing, influencer collaborations, guest blogging, and content syndication to amplify your content's visibility. Leverage your existing networks and engage with industry communities to increase your content's exposure.

Part 3: Engaging Your Audience

1. Encouraging User Interaction:

Invite your audience to engage with your content through comments, social sharing, and discussions. Respond to comments and engage in conversations to foster a sense of community and encourage repeat visits. User-generated content and testimonials can also provide social proof and enhance engagement.

2. Personalization:

Tailor your content to individual users by personalizing their experience. Use data-driven insights to deliver relevant content recommendations, personalized email newsletters, or targeted offers. Personalization helps create a more personalized and engaging experience, increasing customer satisfaction and loyalty.

3. Analyzing and Iterating:

Regularly analyze the performance of your content marketing efforts. Monitor key metrics such as website traffic, engagement rates, conversion rates, and social media metrics. Use this data to identify trends, understand audience preferences, and optimize your content strategy for better results.

Implementing effective content marketing strategies is essential for businesses to thrive in the digital landscape. By understanding your objectives, knowing your audience, and creating valuable and relevant content, you can attract and engage your target audience. Through strategic content creation, diversification of formats, optimization for search engines, and proactive content promotion, you can maximize your content's reach and impact. Finally, by fostering user interaction, personalizing experiences, and analyzing performance, you can continuously refine your content marketing strategies for optimal results. Embrace the power of content marketing to build brand authority, drive customer engagement, and achieve long-term business success.

7.2 Analyzing Website Performance and Making Improvements

Analyzing and improving website performance is crucial for businesses to ensure optimal user experiences, achieve business objectives, and stay competitive in the digital landscape. By understanding key performance metrics, identifying areas for improvement, and implementing effective strategies, businesses can enhance website performance, increase conversions, and drive success. In this guide, we will explore the importance of website performance analysis, key performance indicators (KPIs) to track, and strategies for making improvements.

Part 1: Importance of Website Performance Analysis

1. User Experience and Engagement:

Website performance directly impacts user experience and engagement. Slow page load times, navigation difficulties, and errors can frustrate visitors, leading to high bounce rates and low engagement. Analyzing website performance helps identify pain points and provides insights for enhancing user experiences.

2. Conversion Rates and Revenue:

A well-performing website significantly impacts conversion rates and revenue. Studies show that faster loading times and smoother user experiences positively correlate with higher conversion rates. Analyzing website performance enables businesses to optimize conversion funnels, improve customer journeys, and increase revenue.

3. SEO and Organic Traffic:

Website performance is a crucial factor in search engine optimization (SEO). Search engines consider website speed, mobile-friendliness, and user experience when ranking websites. Analyzing website performance allows businesses to identify and fix issues that may negatively impact SEO rankings and organic traffic.

Part 2: Key Performance Indicators (KPIs) to Track

1. Page Load Time:

Page load time is a critical KPI that directly impacts user experience. Slow loading times can lead to increased bounce rates and decreased engagement. Use tools like Google PageSpeed Insights or GTmetrix to measure and optimize page load times.

2. Mobile Responsiveness:

As mobile usage continues to rise, mobile responsiveness is vital. Monitor your website's performance on different mobile devices and screen sizes. Ensure your website is optimized for mobile users, providing seamless experiences across devices.

3. Conversion Rates:

Track conversion rates to assess the effectiveness of your website in converting visitors into customers or achieving desired actions. Monitor conversion rates for different landing pages, forms, or sales funnels to identify areas for improvement and implement conversion rate optimization (CRO) strategies.

4. Bounce Rate:

The bounce rate indicates the percentage of visitors who leave your website after viewing only one page. A high bounce rate may indicate issues with content relevance, website usability, or slow loading times. Analyze bounce rate data to identify pages that require improvement.

5. Exit Pages:

Exit pages indicate the last pages visitors view before leaving your website. Understanding which pages have the highest exit rates can help identify potential issues or areas for optimization. Evaluate these pages to improve content, navigation, or calls to action.

Part 3: Strategies for Making Website Improvements

1. Website Performance Optimization:

Optimize website performance by compressing images, minifying code, leveraging browser caching, and using content delivery networks (CDNs). Regularly monitor and improve your website's loading speed to enhance user experiences and SEO rankings.

2. User Experience Enhancements:

Analyze user flows, navigation patterns, and heatmaps to identify usability issues. Simplify navigation, improve site structure, and optimize user interfaces to enhance user experiences and increase engagement.

3. A/B Testing and Conversion Rate Optimization (CRO):

Implement A/B testing to compare different versions of web pages, forms, or calls to action. Analyze user behavior, conversion rates, and engagement metrics to optimize conversions and improve the effectiveness of your website elements.

4. Mobile Optimization:

Ensure your website is fully optimized for mobile devices. Implement responsive design, test mobile usability, and optimize mobile-specific features like click-to-call buttons or mobile checkout processes. Mobile optimization enhances user experiences and boosts mobile conversions.

5. Content Optimization:

Evaluate your content's performance by analyzing engagement metrics, time on the page, and scroll depth. Optimize content by improving readability, adding multimedia elements, and making it more relevant to your target audience's needs and preferences.

Analyzing website performance and making improvements is a continuous process that ensures optimal user experiences, drives conversions, and boosts business success. By tracking key performance indicators, addressing pain points, and implementing effective strategies, businesses can enhance website performance, engage their audience, and achieve their goals. Prioritize website optimization, user experience enhancements, and mobile responsiveness to stay ahead in the digital landscape and provide exceptional online experiences for your visitors. Regularly monitor and analyze your website's performance to identify areas for improvement and continue refining your strategies for ongoing success.

7.3 Troubleshooting and Support

In the digital landscape, website issues, and technical glitches can occur, hindering user experiences and impacting business operations. Effective troubleshooting and support processes are essential to quickly identify and resolve these issues, ensuring smooth website functionality and customer satisfaction. In this guide, we will explore key strategies for troubleshooting website problems and providing reliable support to address user concerns.

Part 1: Understanding Common Website Issues

1. Server and Hosting Problems:

Issues related to servers or hosting providers can result in website downtime, slow loading times, or intermittent errors. These problems may arise from server misconfigurations, insufficient resources, or security vulnerabilities.

2. Website Performance and Speed:

Slow loading times, high bounce rates, and poor overall performance can frustrate users and negatively impact SEO rankings. Factors such as unoptimized code, excessive page size, or inadequate server resources can contribute to these issues.

3. Broken Links and 404 Errors:

Broken links and 404 errors occur when users encounter dead-end links or pages that no longer exist. These issues can arise from URL changes, improper redirects, or content removal without proper updates.

Part 2: Troubleshooting Website Issues

1. Monitoring and Error Logging:

Implement monitoring tools to track website performance, uptime, and error logs. This enables proactive identification of issues and provides valuable data for troubleshooting. Tools like Google Analytics, server logs, or specialized website monitoring services can help in this process.

2. Identifying the Root Cause:

When troubleshooting website issues, it's important to identify the root cause. This involves analyzing error messages, reviewing server logs, and conducting systematic tests to isolate the problem. Collaboration between developers, system administrators, and support staff is crucial for efficient troubleshooting.

3. Testing in a Controlled Environment:

When investigating issues, it's recommended to replicate the problem in a controlled environment. This can involve using development or staging environments to isolate and analyze the issue without affecting the live website. Testing allows for targeted troubleshooting and prevents disruptions to user experiences.

4. Debugging and Code Review:

For issues related to custom code or website functionality, debugging and code review play a vital role. Developers can use debugging tools and techniques to identify coding errors, conflicts, or outdated dependencies. Regular code reviews can help identify potential issues before they impact the live website.

Part 3: Providing Effective Support

1. Help Desk and Ticketing Systems:

Implement a help desk or ticketing system to efficiently manage user support requests. This centralized system allows support staff to track, prioritize, and respond to user inquiries promptly. It also helps maintain a record of user issues and resolutions for future reference.

2. Knowledge Base and FAQs:

Develop a comprehensive knowledge base and frequently asked questions (FAQs) section to address common user concerns. This self-service resource provides users with immediate answers and reduces the volume of support requests. Regularly update the knowledge base to reflect evolving user needs and changes to the website.

3. Timely Communication and Status Updates:

Effective communication is crucial in support interactions. Respond to user inquiries promptly, acknowledging their concerns and providing estimated resolution times. Keep users informed of the progress and status of their requests, providing updates on troubleshooting efforts.

4. Empathy and Professionalism:

Approach support interactions with empathy and professionalism. Understand the user's frustration or concerns and provide clear, courteous, and helpful responses. Strive to exceed user expectations by going the extra mile to resolve issues and deliver exceptional support experiences.

5. Continuous Improvement and Feedback:

Regularly review support processes, analyze user feedback, and identify areas for improvement. Encourage users to provide feedback on their support experiences, allowing you to make necessary adjustments and enhancements to the support system and troubleshoot more effectively in the future.

Troubleshooting website issues and providing effective support is crucial for maintaining a seamless online experience for users. By understanding common website issues, implementing systematic troubleshooting processes, and delivering reliable support, businesses can quickly resolve problems, minimize disruptions, and ensure customer satisfaction. Prioritize monitoring, proactive testing, and continuous improvement to enhance website performance, resolve issues promptly, and foster positive user experiences. With a robust troubleshooting and support framework in place, businesses can build trust, loyalty, and long-term relationships with their audience.

Chapter 8: Common WordPress Issues and Solutions

WordPress is a popular content management system used by millions of websites worldwide. While it offers a powerful and flexible platform, users may encounter common issues that can affect website functionality and user experiences. In this guide, we will explore some of the most common WordPress issues and provide practical solutions to help users troubleshoot and resolve these problems effectively.

Part 1: WordPress Installation and Setup Issues

1. White Screen of Death (WSOD):

The "White Screen of Death" occurs when a WordPress website displays a blank white screen, indicating a PHP error. It can be caused by incompatible plugins or themes, memory limit exhaustion, or syntax errors in the code. To resolve this, disable plugins, switch to a default theme, increase memory limits, and check for code errors.

2. Database Connection Errors:

Database connection errors prevent WordPress from accessing the database, resulting in website downtime. These errors may occur due to incorrect database credentials, corrupted database files, or server issues. Verify database credentials, repair the database, and check server configuration to resolve these errors.

3. Permalinks Not Working:

Permalinks define the structure of URLs in WordPress. Sometimes, permalinks may not work properly, resulting in 404 errors or incorrect page URLs. To fix this, go to the Permalinks settings and select a different permalink structure. If that doesn't work, check if the .htaccess file is writable and flush the rewrite rules.

Part 2: Plugin and Theme-Related Issues

1. Plugin Compatibility Issues:

Incompatible plugins can cause conflicts, leading to errors or the malfunctioning of certain website features. Disable recently installed plugins to identify the problematic ones. Update plugins to their latest versions, or contact the plugin developer for support and compatibility information.

2. Theme Compatibility Issues:

Themes may not always be compatible with the latest version of WordPress or other plugins. This can result in visual glitches, broken layouts, or conflicts with certain functionalities. Ensure your theme is regularly updated, or consider switching to a more compatible theme to resolve these issues.

3. Slow Website Performance:

Excessive use of plugins or poorly optimized themes can significantly slow down a WordPress website. Enable caching, minify CSS and JavaScript files, optimize images, and consider using a content delivery network (CDN) to improve website speed. Evaluate and remove unnecessary plugins that may be causing performance issues.

Part 3: Security and Maintenance Issues

1. Website Security Breaches:

WordPress websites can be vulnerable to security breaches if not properly maintained. Common security issues include outdated WordPress versions, insecure plugins or themes, weak passwords, or compromised user accounts. Keep WordPress, themes, and plugins updated, use strong passwords, install security plugins, and regularly scan for malware to enhance website security.

2. Website Backup and Restoration:

A lack of website backups can lead to irretrievable data loss during unforeseen circumstances such as hacking, server failures, or human error. Use reliable backup plugins or services to schedule regular backups of your WordPress website. Additionally, ensure you have a restoration plan in place to recover your website if needed.

3. Maintenance and Updates:

Neglecting regular maintenance tasks can result in website issues and vulnerabilities. Stay up to date with WordPress core updates, theme updates, and plugin updates to access new features, bug fixes, and security patches. Test updates in a staging environment before implementing them on your live website to avoid compatibility issues.

By understanding and addressing common WordPress issues, users can ensure a smooth and functional website experience. Whether its installation and setup issues, plugin or theme conflicts, or security and maintenance concerns, proactive troubleshooting and implementation of the suggested solutions can resolve these issues effectively. Regular updates, backups, and security measures will help maintain a secure and optimized WordPress website. Remember to consult official documentation, seek support from plugin/theme developers or the WordPress community, and utilize reliable resources to troubleshoot and resolve any WordPress-related issues encountered.

8.1 Seeking Help from the WordPress Community

WordPress, being a popular content management system, benefits from a vibrant and supportive community. Whether you're a beginner or an experienced user, there may come a time when you need assistance or have questions regarding your WordPress website. In this guide, we will explore various avenues within the WordPress community where you can seek help, find support, and connect with fellow WordPress enthusiasts.

Part 1: Official WordPress Resources

1. WordPress.org Support Forums:

The WordPress.org Support Forums are a valuable resource for seeking help and finding answers to your WordPress-related queries. These forums are community-driven and host discussions on various topics, including installation, themes, plugins, troubleshooting, and more. You can post your questions and engage with knowledgeable members who are eager to provide assistance.

2. WordPress Documentation:

The official WordPress documentation, available at codex.wordpress.org, provides comprehensive information and tutorials on various aspects of WordPress. It covers topics such as installation, configuration, customization, and plugin development. The documentation is regularly updated and serves as a reliable source of information for both beginners and advanced users.

3. WordPress.org Showcase:

The WordPress.org Showcase is a gallery featuring a wide range of websites built using WordPress. Browsing through the showcase can inspire you with design ideas and provide insights into the capabilities of WordPress. You can also reach out to website owners to inquire about specific features or techniques they have implemented.

Part 2: WordPress Meetups and WordCamps

1. WordPress Meetups:

WordPress Meetups are local, in-person gatherings organized by the WordPress community. These meetups offer opportunities to connect with other WordPress users, developers, designers, and enthusiasts in your area. They often include presentations, discussions, and workshops focused on various WordPress-related topics. Meetup.com and the official WordPress Meetup page (meetup.wordpress.org) are great resources for finding WordPress meetups near you.

2. WordCamps:

WordCamps are larger-scale WordPress events held worldwide, offering a wide range of sessions, workshops, and networking opportunities. These events bring together WordPress professionals and enthusiasts, providing valuable learning experiences and the chance to connect with experts in the field. The official WordCamp website (central.wordcamp.org) provides information on upcoming events and ticket availability.

Part 3: Online Communities and Social Media

1. WordPress Stack Exchange:

WordPress Stack Exchange is a question-and-answer platform where users can ask specific WordPress-related questions and receive answers from the community. The platform follows a voting system where the best answers are recognized and displayed prominently. It's a great resource for finding solutions to technical or specific WordPress issues.

2. WordPress Subreddit:

Reddit hosts a dedicated community at r/WordPress, where users can engage in discussions, seek advice, and share their experiences related to WordPress. It's a platform that encourages interaction and provides a space for users to ask questions and receive helpful responses from the community.

3. WordPress-related Facebook Groups:

Numerous Facebook groups cater to WordPress users, developers, designers, and enthusiasts. These groups offer a platform for sharing knowledge, asking questions, and receiving support. Some popular groups include "Advanced WordPress" and "WordPress Help for Beginners."

Part 4: WordPress Blogs and Podcasts

1. WordPress-focused Blogs:

Several blogs provide valuable insights, tutorials, and tips on WordPress. Websites like WPBeginner, WPExplorer, and WPMU DEV publish informative articles covering various aspects of WordPress. Subscribing to these blogs and regularly reading their content can expand your knowledge and keep you updated with the latest trends and developments in the WordPress ecosystem.

2. WordPress-related Podcasts:

Podcasts such as "The WordPress Chick," "WPwatercooler," and "Matt Report" feature discussions and interviews with WordPress experts, providing valuable insights and industry perspectives. Listening to these podcasts can help you stay informed about WordPress news, trends, and best practices.

The WordPress community is a valuable resource for seeking help, finding support, and connecting with like-minded individuals. Whether you're facing technical issues, seeking advice on customization, or looking to expand your knowledge, the WordPress community offers a range of platforms and resources to assist you. Remember to approach these communities with respect, follow community guidelines, and contribute back whenever possible. By engaging with the WordPress community, you can tap into a wealth of collective expertise and foster meaningful connections within the WordPress ecosystem.

8.2 Engaging Professional WordPress Support Services

WordPress is a powerful and widely used content management system that empowers individuals and businesses to create and manage their websites. However, there may be instances when you require professional help to overcome complex challenges, optimize your website, or ensure its smooth operation. In this guide, we will explore the benefits of engaging professional WordPress support services and provide insights into the various options available to access expert assistance.

Part 1: Why Consider Professional WordPress Support Services

1. Expertise and Experience:

Professional WordPress support services offer access to a team of experts who possess in-depth knowledge and experience in working with WordPress. They are well-versed in troubleshooting common issues, implementing best practices, and optimizing WordPress websites. Their expertise can help you overcome challenges more efficiently and effectively.

2. Time and Cost Savings:

Engaging professional support services can save you valuable time and resources. Instead of spending hours trying to resolve complex issues on their own, professionals can quickly identify and address problems, reducing downtime and minimizing potential revenue loss. Moreover, their expertise can help you avoid costly mistakes and ensure your website operates optimally.

3. Customized Solutions:

Professional support services can provide tailored solutions that address your unique requirements. They can assist with custom development, plugin/theme customization, performance optimization, security audits, and more. Their ability to understand your specific needs ensures that you receive solutions that align with your goals and enhance your website's performance.

Part 2: Types of Professional WordPress Support Services

1. Managed WordPress Hosting Providers:

Many managed WordPress hosting providers offer support services as part of their hosting packages. They provide assistance with website setup, optimization, security, and regular backups. Managed hosting providers have WordPress experts on staff who can handle technical aspects and provide guidance when needed.

2. WordPress Development Agencies:

WordPress development agencies specialize in building and maintaining WordPress websites. They offer a range of services, including theme development, plugin development, website customization, and ongoing maintenance. Working with a development agency can provide access to a team of professionals dedicated to optimizing and enhancing your website.

3. Freelance WordPress Professionals:

Freelance WordPress professionals offer individualized services tailored to your specific needs. They can assist with website setup, customization, troubleshooting, and ongoing support. Hiring a freelance professional can be a cost-effective option for smaller projects or specific tasks that require expertise.

4. WordPress Support Companies:

There are companies solely focused on providing WordPress support services. They offer a range of support options, including on-demand assistance, ticket-based support, and ongoing maintenance plans. These companies have dedicated support teams that can handle various aspects of WordPress management and provide timely solutions.

Part 3: Factors to Consider When Choosing Professional WordPress Support Services

1. Expertise and Specialization:

Evaluate the expertise and specialization of the support service provider. Ensure they have a proven track record of working with WordPress and possess the necessary skills to address your specific requirements.

2. Service Offerings:

Review the service offerings of the support service provider to ensure they align with your needs. Consider factors such as website setup, optimization, security, ongoing maintenance, and customization to determine if their services meet your expectations.

3. Response Time and Availability:

Consider the response time and availability of the support service provider. Prompt and reliable support is crucial, especially during emergencies or critical situations. Look for providers who offer responsive support channels and have a reputation for timely assistance.

4. Client Reviews and Testimonials:

Research client reviews and testimonials to gauge the satisfaction level of previous customers. This can provide insights into the quality of service, professionalism, and expertise of the support service provider.

5. Cost and Value:

Evaluate the cost and value proposition of the support service provider. Compare pricing structures, service levels, and included features to ensure you are getting the best value for your investment.

Engaging professional WordPress support services can be immensely beneficial in ensuring the smooth operation and optimization of your website. Whether you choose a managed hosting provider, a WordPress development agency, a freelance professional, or a dedicated support company, accessing expert assistance can save you time, enhance your website's performance, and provide peace of mind. Consider your specific needs, evaluate the available options, and choose a support service provider that aligns with your requirements and goals. By partnering with professionals, you can leverage their expertise to overcome challenges, optimize your WordPress website, and focus on achieving your online objectives.

Conclusion:

In "Mastering WordPress: A Comprehensive Guide to Building Dynamic Websites for Beginners and Small Business Owners," we have embarked on a journey to equip you with the knowledge and skills to create and manage powerful websites using WordPress. Throughout this book, we have explored various aspects of WordPress, from its fundamentals to advanced customization techniques, with the aim of empowering you to build dynamic and engaging online platforms.

We began by understanding the essence of WordPress and its benefits, recognizing its user-friendly interface and extensive functionality. We then delved into setting up your WordPress environment, navigating the dashboard, and getting started with the platform. We explored the process of installing WordPress on your hosting server, selecting and customizing themes, and creating and managing user accounts.

Building upon this foundation, we delved into planning your website's structure and layout, creating pages, and organizing content effectively. We also covered the importance of essential plugins and demonstrated how to configure them for optimal functionality. Additionally, we explored the art of designing your website and choosing the right theme for your business, ensuring a visually appealing and impactful online presence.

We also recognized the significance of incorporating images and media, enhancing your website's functionality, optimizing it for search engines, and implementing e-commerce capabilities. Moreover, we emphasized the importance of maintaining and securing your website to safeguard its integrity and protect it from potential threats.

Throughout this journey, we highlighted the value of engaging with the WordPress community, seeking support, and leveraging professional assistance when needed. We emphasized the significance of analyzing website performance, engaging with your audience, utilizing social media integration, and implementing effective content marketing strategies to maximize the impact of your website.

Lastly, we discussed troubleshooting common WordPress issues, implementing security measures, and ensuring regular backups to safeguard your website's data and maintain its stability. We also explored the process of updating WordPress, themes, and plugins to stay current with the latest features and security patches.

As we conclude this comprehensive guide, we hope that you have gained a solid understanding of WordPress and the tools necessary to build dynamic websites. Whether you are a beginner or a small business owner, this book has equipped you with the essential knowledge and skills to create, customize, and manage your online presence effectively.

Remember, mastering WordPress is an ongoing journey of continuous learning and exploration. Stay curious, stay updated, and continue to harness the power of WordPress to unleash the full potential of your websites. With dedication, creativity, and the knowledge gained from this guide, you have the tools to create remarkable online experiences that captivate your audience and drive your business forward.

Happy WordPress journey!

Recap of Key Concepts:

Throughout "Mastering WordPress: A Comprehensive Guide to Building Dynamic Websites for Beginners and Small Business Owners," we have covered a wide range of essential concepts and techniques. Let's recap some of the key points covered in this book:

1. WordPress Basics: We started by understanding the fundamentals of WordPress, including its user-friendly interface, flexibility, and robust functionality.
2. Setting Up: We explored the process of setting up a WordPress environment, including choosing a hosting server, installing WordPress, and configuring essential settings.
3. Navigating the Dashboard: We familiarized ourselves with the WordPress dashboard and its various sections, menus, and settings, enabling us to navigate and manage our website effectively.
4. Themes and Customization: We delved into the world of WordPress themes, learning how to choose the right theme for our website and customize its appearance to match our brand identity.
5. User Management: We discussed the importance of creating and managing user accounts, and assigning appropriate roles and permissions to ensure smooth collaboration and website administration.
6. Website Foundation: We emphasized the significance of planning and organizing our website's structure and layout, creating a solid foundation for our content and navigation.
7. Content Creation: We explored the process of creating pages, organizing content effectively, and utilizing different types of media, such as images and videos, to enhance our website's visual appeal.
8. Essential Plugins: We discussed the importance of using plugins to extend the functionality of our website, configuring essential

plugins for tasks such as SEO optimization, security, and contact forms.

9. Website Design: We learned about website design principles and techniques to create visually appealing and engaging websites, focusing on aspects such as layout, color schemes, typography, and branding.

10. Search Engine Optimization (SEO): We covered the basics of optimizing our website for search engines, including keyword research, on-page optimization, and utilizing SEO plugins to improve our website's visibility.

11. E-commerce Functionality: We explored the process of implementing e-commerce functionality on our website, enabling us to sell products or services and manage online transactions securely.

12. Maintenance and Security: We emphasized the importance of regular website maintenance, including updating WordPress, themes, and plugins, performing backups, and implementing security measures to protect our website from potential threats.

13. Engaging our Audience: We discussed strategies for growing our website's audience and engaging them effectively, including social media integration, content marketing, and analyzing website performance.

14. Troubleshooting and Support: We covered common WordPress issues and solutions, and explored the options available for seeking help and support from the WordPress community or professional services.

By understanding and applying these key concepts, you are well-equipped to build dynamic and successful websites using WordPress. Remember, practice and continuous learning are essential to mastering WordPress and staying ahead in the ever-evolving digital landscape. Happy website building!

Next Steps in Mastering WordPress:

Congratulations on completing "Mastering WordPress: A Comprehensive Guide to Building Dynamic Websites for Beginners and Small Business Owners"! By now, you have acquired a solid foundation in WordPress and have the necessary knowledge and skills to create and manage your website effectively. But the journey doesn't end here. To continue mastering WordPress, consider the following next steps:

1. Stay Updated: WordPress is constantly evolving, with new features, updates, and trends emerging regularly. Stay updated by following WordPress news, blogs, and official documentation. Engage with the WordPress community and attend WordCamps or local meetups to stay abreast of the latest developments.
2. Explore Advanced Techniques: Now that you have a strong understanding of WordPress basics, consider diving deeper into more advanced techniques. Explore custom theme development, plugin development, and advanced customization options to take your website to the next level.
3. Experiment and Test: WordPress offers a vast ecosystem of themes, plugins, and integrations. Experiment with different combinations and configurations to discover what works best for your website. Test different strategies, layouts, and content to optimize user experience and achieve your website's goals.
4. Expand Your Skill Set: Consider expanding your skill set beyond WordPress. Explore related technologies like HTML, CSS, JavaScript, and PHP, which will enhance your ability to customize and extend the functionality of your website. Additionally, learning about web design principles, user experience (UX) design, and digital marketing will complement your WordPress expertise.

5. Join WordPress Communities: Engage with the vibrant WordPress community to network with like-minded individuals, seek advice, and share your knowledge. Join online forums, participate in discussions, and contribute to the community through support forums or by sharing your experiences and insights.

6. Continuously Learn: The world of technology is ever-evolving, and WordPress is no exception. Stay curious and embrace a mindset of continuous learning. Explore online tutorials, video courses, and resources to expand your knowledge. Consider enrolling in advanced WordPress courses or pursuing certifications to enhance your professional credentials.

7. Build Real-World Projects: Apply your WordPress skills to real-world projects. Whether it's creating a website for a client, starting a personal blog, or launching an e-commerce store, hands-on experience will solidify your understanding and help you discover new challenges and opportunities.

8. Share Your Expertise: As you continue to grow and master WordPress, consider sharing your expertise with others. Start a blog, create tutorials, or contribute to the WordPress community by writing documentation or translating resources. Sharing your knowledge not only helps others but also reinforces your understanding of WordPress concepts.

Remember, mastering WordPress is an ongoing process that requires dedication, practice, and a commitment to continuous learning. Embrace new challenges, keep experimenting, and leverage the power of WordPress to create remarkable websites that make an impact. Enjoy your journey as you further develop your WordPress skills and become a proficient WordPress developer and website owner!

www.ingramcontent.com/pod-product-compliance
Lightning Source LLC
LaVergne TN
LVHW081528050326
832903LV00025B/1676